AS Sociology

UNIT 2

AQA

Module 2: Education

Emma Jones & Marsha Jones

For Lola

Philip Allan Updates
Market Place
Deddington
Oxfordshire
OX15 0SE

Tel: 01869 338652
Fax: 01869 337590
e-mail: sales@philipallan.co.uk
www.philipallan.co.uk

ISBN 0 86003 464 X

This Guide has been written specifically to support students preparing for the AQA AS Sociology Unit 2 examination. The content has been neither approved nor endorsed by AQA and remains the sole responsibility of the authors.

Printed by Information Press, Eynsham, Oxford

Contents

Introduction

Content Guidance

Questions and Answers

Introduction

About this guide

This unit guide is for students following the AQA AS Sociology course. It deals with the Module 2 topic **Education**, which is examined within Unit 2. It provides an overview of the main areas within the topic, but you should also make sure that you are familiar with the subject matter as given by your teachers. There are three sections to this guide:

- **Introduction** — this provides advice on how to use this unit guide, guidance on revision and an outline of the assessment aims of AS Sociology. It concludes with guidance on how to succeed in the unit test.
- **Content Guidance** — this provides details of the specification subsections of Education. (The exam question on Education can be about any aspect within the specification, so do not leave any areas out.) Each topic area examines **key ideas**, stating the main points of evaluation and listing the key concepts and thinkers.
- **Questions and Answers** — this shows you the kind of questions you can expect in the unit test. The first five questions are followed by two sample answers (an A-grade and a C-grade response). These are interspersed with examiner comments so that you can see how the marks are allocated. The sixth question is for you to attempt yourself.

How to use the guide

To use this guide to your best advantage, you should refer to the Introduction and Content Guidance sections from the beginning of your study of Education. However, in order to get full advantage from the Question and Answer section, you would be advised to wait until you have completed your study of the topic, as the questions are wide-ranging. When you are ready to use this section, you should take each question in turn, study it carefully, and either write a full answer yourself or, at the very least, answer parts (a) to (d) fully and write a plan for parts (e) and (f). When you have done this, study the grade-A candidate's answer and compare it with your own, paying close attention to the examiner's comments. You could also look at the grade-C answers and, using the examiner's comments as a guide, work out how to rewrite them to gain higher marks.

These tasks are quite intensive and time-consuming, and you should not be tempted to try to tackle all the questions in a short space of time. It is better to focus on one at a time, and spread the workload over several weeks — you can always find some time to do this, even while studying another topic. In addition to using the questions to consolidate your own knowledge and develop your exam skills, you should use at least some of the questions as revision practice — even just reading through the grade-A candidates' answers should provide you with useful revision material.

The AS specification

The aims of the AS Sociology course are to enable you to:
- acquire knowledge and a critical understanding of contemporary social processes and structures
- appreciate the significance of theoretical and conceptual issues in sociological debate
- understand sociological methodology and a range of research methods
- reflect on your own experience of the social world in which you live
- develop skills which enhance your ability to participate more effectively in adult life

Examinable skills

AS Sociology papers are designed to test certain skills. These skills, or 'Assessment Objectives', are common to both AS and A2, but their weighting differs. There are two main Assessment Objectives in the specification, and each counts for half of the available marks.

The first of the Assessment Objectives (AO1) is 'knowledge and understanding', which must be clearly communicated to the examiners. Knowledge and understanding are linked together, indicating that you must not only demonstrate possession of sociological knowledge but also be able to use it in a meaningful way. Understanding implies that you can select appropriate knowledge and use it in answer to a specific question. The skill of knowledge and understanding covers the following aspects of sociological thought:
- social order
- social control
- social change
- conflict and consensus
- social structure and social action
- macro- and micro-perspectives
- the nature of social facts
- the role of values
- the relationship between sociology and social policy

AS candidates are also required to study two core themes:
- socialisation, culture and identity
- social differentiation, power and stratification

These themes are to be applied to the topic areas in the specification and not tested as separate topics. You will see how these two core themes can be applied to the topic of Education as you read this guide.

Assessment Objective 2 (AO2) covers 'identification, analysis, interpretation and evaluation'. You must learn to:

- **identify** appropriate pieces of knowledge
- **distinguish** between facts and opinions
- **analyse** research methods and research studies in terms of their strengths and weaknesses
- **interpret** material such as research findings and statistics in order to identify any trends and uncover the (sometimes hidden) meanings
- and, perhaps most importantly of all, show the ability to **evaluate**

The skill of evaluation is an important one, and should be applied to all the material you come across during your study of a topic. In practice, this means that you should develop the habit of asking questions, such as 'Who says so?', 'How did they find that out?', 'Is there any other evidence of this?', 'Who does not agree with this view?', and so on. In perhaps more practical terms, it means that whenever you are introduced to a sociological perspective or study, you should find and learn at least *two* criticisms that have been made of it. You should also note, of course, which group or person has made these criticisms, as this is an important piece of information.

In addition to the above skills, you must:

- be well organised so that your arguments are coherent
- show an awareness of the theoretical debates in sociology
- use evidence to support and sustain your arguments and conclusions

Study skills and revision strategies

- Good revision equals good results and needs time spent on it.
- As well as reading and making notes, you should try to read a quality newspaper such as the *Guardian*, the *Independent* or the *Observer* at least once a week. The *Guardian* has sections dedicated to society, media and education that are of particular sociological interest. They will provide you with contemporary examples that you can refer to in your essays.
- Surf the net! There are now some excellent websites dedicated to AS and A-level Sociology.
- If you do not already subscribe to *Sociology Review*, your school or college library probably does. Read back copies. This magazine is invaluable for keeping you up to date with sociological research and for giving good advice on exams.
- For each of your AS units, make sure that you know what the examination board specifies as necessary knowledge. Make notes on each of these areas and keep them in a revision folder separate from your class notes.
- Be organised! Make yourself an examination and revision timetable, divided into topics, at least *2 months* before the exams start.
- When you finally reach the week(s) of the exams, get a good night's sleep each

night. Do *not* stay up until the early hours trying to get in some last-minute revision.
- In the exam, allocate your time carefully. Make sure that you have enough time to write the *two* essays as well as answer the shorter questions.

The unit test

Education is a Module 2 topic. This module also contains the topics of Wealth, Poverty and Welfare, and Work and Leisure. The unit test will contain three questions, one on each of these three topics, and you will have to answer one question in the examination time of $1\frac{1}{4}$ hours. The unit as a whole is worth 35% of the AS qualification and $17\frac{1}{2}$% of the total A-level qualification. Each question is marked out of 60, and of the 60 marks, 30 are given to AO1 (knowledge and understanding) and 30 to AO2 (identification, analysis, interpretation and evaluation).

Each question in the examination will feature source material, or 'items' — usually two of them. These are designed to help you by providing information on which you may draw in your answer. It is therefore essential that before attempting to answer any part of the question, you read the items carefully, and continue to refer to them throughout the examination. Sometimes a question will make a specific reference to an item, such as 'With reference to Item A', or 'Using evidence from Item B and elsewhere'. In these cases you should make quite sure that you clearly follow the instruction. An easy way of doing this is to say, for example, 'The view referred to in Item A is that...', 'Item A shows evidence of...', 'Item B gives examples of...' or 'The view in Item B reflects the Marxist view of..., which has been criticised, particularly by functionalists, who argue that...'.

Each question is broken down into a number of parts, usually (a) to (f), each with its own mark allocation. The first series of questions, typically (a) to (d), will together add up to 20 marks, and require short answers. As is usual in such cases, the higher the mark allocation, the more you would normally need to write to gain full marks. The remaining parts, (e) and (f), each carry 20 marks, and there is an important difference between them with regard to the balance of the two assessment objectives.

Part (e) is weighted towards knowledge and understanding, which carries 14 of the 20 available marks, leaving 6 marks for the remaining skills. This means that in answering this question, you should ensure that you show evidence of appropriate sociological knowledge and understanding. Remember, though, that 6 marks are for demonstration of the remaining skills, so these, particularly evaluation, should not be neglected. You should therefore make sure that you include some critical or evaluative comments at suitable points in your answer.

In part (f) the skills balance is reversed, that is, 14 of the 20 marks are awarded for the skills of identification, analysis, interpretation and evaluation, with 6 marks available for knowledge and understanding. As it is most unlikely that you would be able to demonstrate the AO2 skills without at the same time showing evidence of knowledge and understanding, your focus should be on showing sufficient evidence of the AO2 skills. You will be reminded of this by the wording of the question, which will usually ask you to 'assess' or 'evaluate' something.

Content Guidance

This section is intended to show you the major issues and themes covered in **Education**. Remember, though, that these are offered as guidance only — the lists are neither exhaustive nor exclusive, that is, there are other concepts that are useful and many other studies that are relevant. With regard to studies, whatever textbook you use will contain sufficient examples for your needs, and your teacher will undoubtedly refer you to others. If you have back copies of *Sociology Review* or *S Magazine* in your library, you will also find a number of useful articles on this area of the course. In addition to 'studies', i.e. pieces of sociological research, there are many useful books and articles in which sociologists discuss their ideas about an aspect of education. These will be referred to in your textbooks.

The content of **Education** falls into four main areas:
- **perspectives on education**
- **sociological explanations of the different educational achievements of social groups**
- **education and subcultures**
- **state policies on education**

The AQA AS topic of **Education** is designed to give you a good understanding of the historical development of education and its importance within society today. You will be expected to be familiar with different explanations of the role of the education system. This will include perspectives on education including functionalist, Marxist, feminist and New Right etc. You will also be expected to discuss different explanations of the differing educational achievement of social groups by social class, gender and ethnicity and be familiar with the empirical evidence for these. Another important area will be what happens within schools, with particular reference to teacher–pupil relationships, pupil subcultures, the hidden curriculum and the organisation of teaching and learning. The other major section in this topic is the significance of state policies for an understanding of the role, impact and experience of education. When you have covered all these areas you will have completed the topic. The core themes are integrated within the topic and you will not have to do any extra work on them.

Perspectives on education

Functionalist

Key ideas

- Education is the main agency of secondary socialisation. It takes over as the focal socialising agency after the family. Children are socialised into value consensus.
- Education provides a bridge between the home and the wider society. In school, children are judged by the universalistic standards of society rather than the particularistic values of the home.
- Education is a meritocracy. This means that it acts as a neutral filter ensuring that all pupils receive education suited to their natural aptitudes.
- Education performs the vital task of role allocation. The most able and talented must be filtered into the most functionally important positions in society.
- It reinforces social solidarity in society.

Evaluation

- + Identifies education as an integral part of the social structure.
- + Acknowledges the vital role of education as an agency of secondary socialisation.
- + Identifies the needs of modern industrial societies to have an appropriately skilled workforce produced by the education system.
- − Marxists argue that:
  - meritocracy is a myth
  - education transmits the values and ideology of the dominant class
  - education reproduces the next generation of workers for capitalism

Key concepts

meritocracy; role allocation; secondary socialisation; social solidarity; transmission of shared norms and values

Key thinkers

Durkheim, Parsons, Davis and Moore.

Marxist

Key ideas

- Meritocracy is a myth.
- Education is a major agency of social control in modern capitalist society.
- Education is an ideological state apparatus that brainwashes children into docility and obedience.
- The hidden curriculum ensures that the values and ideology of the dominant class are internalised as natural and normal by pupils.

- Education reproduces the next generation of workers for capitalism.
- The relationship between teachers and pupils mirrors the exploitative relationship between bosses and workers.
- The economic infrastructure exerts considerable influence over the schooling system. There is a close correspondence between the needs of capitalism and the schooling system.
- The class system is reproduced through the schooling system. Educational inequality is systematic and the real task of the schooling system is to filter working-class pupils into working-class jobs. Middle-class pupils are filtered into the professions.

Evaluation

+ Identifies the education system as shaped by structural factors. Recognises the influence of the economy in the direction of schooling.
+ Much sociological research supports the Marxist claim that working-class pupils are not encouraged to succeed in school.
+ Recognises the importance of ideology in education.
+ Identifies the myth of meritocracy.
− The focus is too class-based. Gender and ethnicity tend to be ignored.
− Overemphasises docility and obedience from pupils. Bowles and Gintis, as well as Althusser, have tended to underestimate pupil resistance to teachers and school.
− Overstates the close connection between the needs of capitalism and the type of school system.

Key concepts

cultural capital; cultural reproduction; hidden curriculum; ideological state apparatus; myth of meritocracy; reproduction of workers for capitalism; social control

Key thinkers

Bowles and Gintis, Bourdieu, Boudon, Althusser, Willis, Braverman.

Feminist

Key ideas

- Education reproduces patriarchal power in society.
- The curriculum is still biased in favour of white middle-class male knowledge.
- Textbooks and reading schemes still have a male bias.
- Teachers give boys more classroom attention.
- The hidden curriculum reinforces gender socialisation.
- Subject choice in secondary school is still gendered.
- Sexual harassment of girls and women teachers by male pupils is a major feature of mixed schools.
- Despite the introduction of the National Curriculum, gender stereotyping in education is still widespread.

+ Identifies the education system as a major agency of gender socialisation.
+ Identifies gender as a key factor in educational inequality.
+ Feminist studies indicate that boys demand and receive more teacher time than girls.
+ Identifies the fact that power in society is patriarchal.
− Traditional feminist explanations have ignored the recent success of girls in schools.
− Boys are now viewed as the underachievers.
− Girls' attitudes have changed towards the importance of education (see Sharpe's study).

Key concepts

gender socialisation; male domination of the classroom; patriarchal curriculum; sexual harassment; subject choice

Key thinkers

Sharpe, Spender, Kelly, Stanworth, Deem, Jones and Mahony, Delamont, Lees.

The New Right

Key ideas

- Market forces should be introduced into schooling. Successful schools are rewarded with increased budgets to increase their roll while failing schools are closed down. Schools are encouraged to compete in the market place for clients (i.e. pupils).
- There is an increased focus on vocational education and preparing pupils for the world of work. This is being achieved by the introduction of general national vocational qualifications (GNVQs), compulsory work experience for year 10 pupils and the National Record of Achievement (NRA) for all year 11 pupils.
- The introduction of national testing at the various key stages.
- The publication of league tables to show standards in schools.
- Schools should have greater control over their budgets and less involvement with the local education authority (LEA).
- Parents should have the right to send their child to the school of their choice.
- A greater focus on school inspection to ensure rising standards in all state schools.

Evaluation

− Stephen Ball et al. argue that New Right reforms to education have served to make education less egalitarian and far more divisive because they give an advantage to middle-class parents. This is because middle-class parents have cultural capital and are therefore more likely to make a favourable impression on the head teacher at interview. Also they understand the schooling system and they can afford to move into a middle-class catchment area where there is a successful school high in the league tables.

– Marxists such as Finn argue that the focus on new vocationalism and youth training is simply reproducing young workers for capitalism who have been socialised into the right attitudes and are ready for exploitation.

Key concepts

competition; league tables; marketisation of education; parental choice; pupil testing; vocationalism

Key thinkers

Chubb and Moe.

Interactionist

Key ideas

- Interactionists examine education from a micro-perspective. The focus is on the day-to-day running of schools and the interaction between teachers and pupils within the classroom.
- The classroom is constructed and constantly renegotiated through interaction between teachers and pupils. Pupils are not passive recipients of teachers' knowledge but actively participate in learning and resistance.
- Teachers play a crucial role in the success of their students. They affect their self-concept and their self-esteem.
- The labelling and typing of students by teachers leads to the creation of self-fulfilling prophecies.
- Streaming and setting have significant effects on the success of pupils in school. There is a close relationship between banding and the social-class background of pupils.
- Pupils resist the school system. This resistance takes different forms, varying from active rebellion and aggression to subtle adaptations of behaviour.

Evaluation

+ Interactionists have challenged the rather deterministic approaches of Marxism and functionalism to education.
+ They have provided valuable insights into the day-to-day running of schools and the reality of the classroom.
+ They have demonstrated the importance of teachers in the success or failure of their pupils.
– Interactionists have been accused of determinism in their approach to education. They presume that once a label has been applied to somebody, a self-fulfilling prophecy will follow.
– The narrow focus on interaction within the school ignores the importance of wider structural constraints in educational success.
– Many ethnographic studies tend to be descriptive rather than explanatory.

interaction; labelling; negotiation; pupil adaptations; pupil subcultures; self-concept; self-fulfilling prophecy; typing

Key thinkers
Becker, Hargreaves, Hester and Mellor, Keddie, Rosenthal and Jacobson, Woods, Ball.

Sociological explanations of the different educational achievements of social groups

This is a large area within the topic of Education and is likely to produce a variety of questions on the examination paper. It is extremely important to be aware of the factors that affect differential achievement. These include **gender**, **ethnicity** and **social-class background**.

Other significant factors affecting underachievement lie within schools themselves. These will be dealt with elsewhere in the guide.

Gender

Gender issues before 1980

- Sociological explanations of gender and educational achievement before the 1980s focused on the underachievement of girls.
- The educational ideology reflected that of the wider, patriarchal society which emphasised the domestic role of women. As a result, many girls (apart from a few who went on to be university-educated) were encouraged to take up those subjects that would fit them for their roles as wives and mothers.
- Goldstein argued that the selection for the tripartite system by 11-plus examination was not an equitable system, as many grammar school places which should have been taken by girls were given to boys in order to even up the numbers of boy and girl pupils. Girls' results were weighted downwards to give boys an equal chance of a grammar school place.
- The career aspirations of girls were seen as less significant than those of boys.
- Socialisation practices at home were seen as detrimental to the career prospects of girls. Gender socialisation encouraged passivity and gentleness in girls and aggression and an instrumental attitude in boys.

- Research into school socialisation focused on reading schemes (Lobban) and discovered a considerable amount of gender-stereotyped material.

Gender issues after 1980

- Over the past two decades, there has been a significant increase in the achievement of girls, especially at GCSE. In 2000, girls were ahead of boys at A-level as well and the gap between the genders had increased. New explanations have been put forward as to why this reversal of fortunes has taken place and the focus has changed to explaining the underachievement of boys.
- Although girls have overtaken boys in public examinations, gender differences in subject choices remain. This is most apparent in science and technology, which are chosen by more boys than girls.
- In higher education there are also changes. In 1996/97 men were more likely to gain first degrees in sciences (other than social and biological sciences) engineering and architecture, building and planning. However, in all but a minority of other subjects, women predominated. Women have now overtaken men in medicine, dentistry, business and finance degrees.
- Colley (1998) found that despite the National Curriculum there are still significant gender differences remaining in option choices. She argues that this is affected by the students' perceptions of subjects.

In-school factors affecting female achievement

- State initiatives in the early 1980s were directed at the enhancement of girls' achievement. Examples include WISE (women into science and engineering), GIST (girls into science and technology) and some of the early Technical and Vocational Educational Initiative (TVEI) programmes.
- The increase in service-sector jobs has enhanced the opportunities for women.
- The women's movement and feminism may have influenced the aspirations of girls and the increasing independence of women may have filtered down into schools.
- The introduction of coursework was said to help girls as they had different study skills to boys.
- The introduction of the National Curriculum ensured that girls could no longer drop out of traditionally masculine subjects like science and mathematics.

Out-of-school factors affecting males and females

- Changes in attitudes: the introduction of a laddish culture (including magazines for young men and the rise of football chat shows on television) which views schoolwork as 'uncool'.
- Changes in the labour market: an increase in unemployment for young men, together with the decline of traditional manufacturing industries.
- Changes in the family: increased divorce and lone parenting has led to a lack of effective role models for boys and encouraged the idea of economic independence for young women.

THE HEALEY COLLEGE LIBRARY

- Gender issues are affected by class and ethnicity too, as some social groups, especially Chinese, African and middle-class Asian girls, achieve much higher standards than others.

Key concepts

femininity/masculinity; feminism; gender socialisation; laddism; malestream; nature vs nurture; patriarchy; sexism

Key thinkers

Sharpe, Stanworth, Deem, Spender, Kelly, Delamont, Rutherford, Mac an Ghaill.

Ethnicity

While it is true that some ethnic minorities underachieve in the British education system, it is a mistaken generalisation to argue that all ethnic minorities underachieve. The highest achievers in terms of educational qualifications are students from Indian and Chinese backgrounds and Asian students from East African backgrounds.

There are three broad explanations for the differing attainment of ethnic minorities in the education system: **genetic explanations (non-sociological)**, **inside-school explanations** and **outside-school explanations**.

Genetic explanations

Genetic explanations start with the premise that intelligence is largely inherited and therefore fixed. It is very important to understand that these views are highly criticised by sociologists. On the basis of IQ tests, psychologists such as Jenson and Eysenck have argued that Black people have less inherited intelligence than Whites. They have been criticised for legitimising racial inequality. Understandably their work has been strongly challenged by sociologists who argue that it is impossible to isolate inheritance from environmental factors such as poverty and racism. For some students these are far more important in relation to their educational success. It is impossible to equalise environmental factors because black people have experienced centuries of racist oppression. Despite having been rejected by sociologists, these genetic explanations still remain.

Inside-school explanations

Curriculum bias and ethnocentrism

Subjects such as English literature, history and religious education have been accused of being ethnocentric. The foci of these subjects have tended to be the achievements of White European (Christian) peoples. The National Curriculum does not include the history of Black people, and foreign languages taught in school are primarily European. Where other languages are taught these tend to be extra-curricular.

Teacher expectations

Much research has indicated that teachers have lower expectations of Black boys than they have of other pupils. These tend to be stereotyped as troublemakers and seen as disruptive. Some sociologists would argue that this labelling is likely to result in a self-fulfilling prophecy.

Institutional racism

In 1999, Ofsted published a damning report on British education claiming that there was institutional racism within the system. (An institution is described as institutionally racist if its policies and personnel discriminate against a particular minority group.) This claim echoed earlier criticisms expressed in the 1985 Swann Report, which claimed that unintentional racism was a feature of many schools. In the 1970s Bernard Coard argued that the British education system made Black pupils 'educationally subnormal'. He argued that the system diminished the self-esteem of Black children. Sociologists have also pointed to the lack of senior Black personnel in education. There is a marked lack of Black head teachers in British schools.

Pupil exclusions

Statistics indicate that all pupil exclusions have risen markedly since the 1980s. This may be due to a range of factors including the focus on school league tables and the reduction in specialist support for pupils with behavioural and learning difficulties. However, Afro-Caribbean pupils are significantly over-represented in exclusion figures. Explanations focus on teacher attitudes, i.e. seeing Black pupils as more disruptive, and on Black pupils expressing their frustration in the classroom at the effects of poverty and racism.

Outside-school explanations

Racism

It is impossible to isolate racism in the school from the experience of living in a racist society. All pupils from Black, Asian and refugee backgrounds face the threat of racial abuse and attack in Britain. Victimisation studies indicate that Asians are 50 times more likely to be the victims of a racist attack than White people, while Black people are 36 times more likely to be victims.

Home factors and parental interest

Cultural deprivation models have placed the blame for educational underachievement on the home. Afro-Caribbean home life has been stereotyped as more stressful, with higher proportions of lone parents and lower family incomes. Pryce claimed that family life among West Indians in Bristol was 'turbulent'. In contrast, Asian families are seen to be a positive resource for their children, with greater emphasis on educational success.

Language factors

In the past, language factors were seen to be significant constraints for both Afro-Caribbean and Asian pupils. It was claimed that pupils coming from homes where

English was not the first language were disadvantaged. However, recent research by Driver and Ballard rejects this explanation and the Swann Report did not emphasise this view.

Social class

It is well documented that differences in social class affect the educational attainment of pupils. There are marked socioeconomic differences between ethnic minorities in Britain. The Swann Report identified socioeconomic factors as being important in the underachievement of West Indian children.

Criticisms/racism reconsidered

Fuller's research showed that Black girls did not accept negative teacher expectations and that they fought the labels to achieve success. Stone's research questioned the view that Black pupils have low self-esteem. Many pupils in the study were hostile to teachers yet maintained a positive self-image.

Prejudice among teachers might be expressed in the staff room but might not necessarily extend into the classroom.

Key concepts

labelling and the self-fulfilling prophecy; ethnocentrism; institutional racism; resistance; curriculum bias

Key thinkers

Wright, Coard, Fuller, Mirza, Pilkington, Brittan, Driver and Ballard, Pryce, Mac an Ghaill.

Social class

Outside-school explanations

Poverty and material deprivation

Poverty and low income are likely to result in fewer books and educational toys in the home. There may be overcrowding and children will have no adequate study area at home. Poverty might result in damp homes that can lead to bronchial infections, more illness and increased time off school. Structural material explanations for inequalities in health see material deprivation as a key factor. Jesson and Gray's 1991 Nottinghamshire study identified a clear correlation between poverty and material deprivation. Half of the pupils receiving free school meals attained GCSE scores below 15 points as opposed to one sixth of pupils who paid for meals.

Home factors and parental interest

Douglas saw parental interest as the single most important factor affecting pupil progress. He argued that in general, middle-class parents were more interested in the progress of their children than were working-class parents. Parental interest was measured by visits to the school and how teachers viewed parents. However, this approach has been criticised for failing to take into account different work practices of parents.

Culture clash

Cultural deficit theorists have maintained that working-class families place great emphasis on immediate gratification and the need to find employment at school leaving age, whereas middle-class families place most emphasis on educational success and staying on post-16. Some working-class pupils may face a culture clash between the values of home and school.

Language difference

Bernstein identified two different speech codes: the **elaborated** and **restricted** codes. He argued that working-class pupils are generally socialised into a restricted language code where meanings are context-bound and sentences short with limited vocabulary. In contrast, the language of the school and teachers is of an elaborated nature.

Cultural capital

According to Bourdieu, inequalities in power and wealth in society account for the inequalities in educational achievement. Bourdieu argues that children from middle- and upper-class backgrounds have been socialised into the dominant culture and possess cultural capital. Their preschool socialisation has been much closer to the dominant culture and the values of the school than that of working-class children. The dominant class has the power to impose its culture and values as legitimate and the curriculum reflects these values and interests. Working-class children are filtered out of the education system at school leaving age through two processes: failure in examinations and self-elimination. They give up on school because it is so alien to them.

Positional theory

Marxist sociologist Raymond Boudon argues that educational inequality is inevitable because of social stratification. Students start school from very different positions, depending on their class. Boudon refers to a cost–benefit analysis of education, whereby studying for higher education may have very different consequences for a middle-class than for a working-class student. The parents of middle-class students are much more likely to be able to support them financially and to encourage them to follow a profession. However, working-class parents are far less likely to have the material resources to support their son or daughter through university. University fees currently exceed £1200 per annum. A working-class student who goes to university, particularly Oxford or Cambridge, will also encounter a significantly different culture from that of home. Working-class students might therefore resist or reject higher education.

Inside-school explanations

Labelling and self-fulfilling prophecy

Teachers are middle class by virtue of their profession and will generally support middle-class values and attitudes. These values may well be at odds with those of some working-class children. Becker's work demonstrated that teachers tended to see middle-class pupils as those closer to the ideal. Keddie's work showed that social class and streaming are closely linked. Pupils from lower working-class backgrounds were predominantly found in lower streams at school. Teachers withheld knowledge that was essential for success from these groups, believing that these students could not handle such complex knowledge. Teachers might stereotype working-class pupils as unlikely to stay on and therefore have lower expectations of these pupils. This may well lead to a self-fulfilling prophecy whereby those children will become disinterested and give up on education.

Key concepts

economic capital; cultural capital; elaborated and restricted language codes; immediate and deferred gratification; fatalism; cultural reproduction; meritocracy

Key thinkers

Halsey, Bernstein, Douglas, Bourdieu, Ball, Keddie, Sugarman, Hyman, Willis, Becker, Rist, Boudon.

Education and subcultures

Key ideas

- Subcultures are created through processes within the school such as streaming and labelling.
- Teachers label lower-stream students as 'failures'. The students attempt to protect their self-identity and self-worth by forming subcultures. Understanding the development of subcultures tends to come from the interactionist approach.
- Early theorists like Cohen and Miller explained the creation of subcultures as resulting from status frustration and the focal concerns of working-class boys. It was assumed that as they were unlikely to be successful within the education system, they would find status outside the school.
- Later researchers such as Woods have argued that pupils' adaptations to the experience of school life depend on acceptance or rejection of the importance of academic success. Woods has identified eight adaptations: ingratiation, compliance, opportunism, ritualism, retreatism, colonisation, intransigence and rebellion. He has related these adaptations to social class by arguing that middle-class students tend to have the more conformist adaptations, whereas the least conformist adaptations are shown by working-class pupils.

Resistance and failure

Willis, from a Marxist perspective, identified two discernible subcultures: the 'lads' and the 'ear'oles'. The lads accorded no value to the education system and qualifications but felt themselves to be superior to the ear'oles who were prepared to be compliant in school in order to gain skilled employment later. Although the lads claimed to resist and 'have a laff at' the system, ironically it was preparing them for low-skilled manual work.

Resistance and success

Fuller's study of a group of Afro-Caribbean girls in a London comprehensive demonstrated another form of resistance. The girls, labelled as failures by their teacher, rejected the negative label and worked hard to ensure their success. Fuller's work is important in showing that subcultural resistance does not necessarily mean academic failure.

> **Evaluation**
> - This takes a relatively deterministic approach to the development of subcultures. It is possible that at times the more conformist pupils will become deviant and disruptive if teachers are seen to be lacking classroom discipline.
> - Not all teachers adopt a middle-class view of the world and might be more sympathetic to the anti-authoritarianism of some pupils.

> **Key concepts**

delinquent subcultures; labelling; resistance; self-fulfilling prophecy; streaming

Key thinkers

Hargreaves, Woods, Willis, Fuller, Mac an Ghaill.

State policies on education

1870 Education Act

The 1870 Forster Act introduced elementary education for all 5- to 10-year-olds. By 1880 it was compulsory for all children to be educated to the age of 10. A limited curriculum was offered focusing on the importance of the 'four Rs': reading, writing, arithmetic and religion.

Over the twentieth century the school leaving age was gradually raised to 16 years. However, social class and education were clearly linked. Until the Second World War, there were three broad types of school, according to social class:
- elementary schools for the working class
- grammar schools for the middle classes (these were fee-paying institutions)
- public schools for the upper classes

1944 Education Act

The 1944 Butler Act was a fundamental part of the creation of the welfare state and introduced free state education for all pupils in England and Wales from the age of 5 up to 15 years. The aim of the Act was to provide equality of educational opportunity for all children, regardless of their socioeconomic background. The act introduced the **tripartite system** whereby all state pupils took an IQ test at 11. On the basis of this test, pupils were allocated to one of three types of secondary school: **grammar**, **secondary modern** or **technical**.

Grammar schools

These were intended for the academically able and were modelled on the public schools. Grammar schools taught the classics and prepared students for higher education. Only 20% of the school population attended grammar school and their intake was predominantly middle class. Pupils had to 'pass' the 11-plus exam to attend a grammar school. The rest of the school population ('11-plus failures') attended either secondary modern or technical schools.

Secondary modern schools

Approximately 75–80% of children attended this type of school, which offered a basic education and little opportunity to take external exams. Approximately 80% of secondary modern pupils left without any qualifications.

Technical schools

These schools emphasised vocational subjects and technical skills. There were very few technical schools built and they were attended by only 5% of the school population.

Criticisms of the tripartite system

Parity of esteem

The tripartite system was founded on the idea of separate but equal types of school for the different aptitudes and abilities of students. However, in reality grammar schools were afforded much higher status than the other schools. Few technical schools were built and the system was really bipartite rather than tripartite.

Low self-esteem

The system resulted in educational success or failure at age 11. Failing the 11-plus created low self-esteem in children and turned them off schooling at an early age. Sociologists argue that once labelled a failure at 11 this created a self-fulfilling prophecy. The 11-plus system was responsible for wastage of educational talent, since the majority of secondary modern students left school with no qualifications.

IQ tests

Sociologists are highly critical of the validity of IQ testing. They believe that these tests are not valid indicators of intelligence but are culturally biased and ethnocentric. The founder of the 11-plus tests, Sir Cyril Burt, was later discovered to have fraudulently created test results to prove his theories that boys were more able than girls and Black people less able than White people.

Social class

Although the system was designed to remove class barriers to education and ensure that every pupil went to the school best suited to his or her aptitudes, in reality there was a very strong correlation between social class and secondary school. Grammar schools were for the most part middle-class institutions, leaving working-class children to a second-rate education in a secondary modern.

Comprehensivisation

By the 1960s, concerns were being raised that the tripartite system had not achieved its aim to democratise education and that the class system was still very much intact. The goal of the tripartite system to produce a meritocracy had failed. In response, the Labour government proposed the introduction of comprehensive schools, which were designed to introduce more social mixing and eradicate testing at 11. In 1965, the Labour government required all LEAs to become comprehensive. This was a very slow business and one that was opposed by the Conservatives. However, by 1974, 80% of secondary pupils attended a comprehensive school.

Criticisms of comprehensivisation

- Standards have been lowered and higher-ability children have been held back.
- Comprehensivisation has not succeeded in more social mixing. Class differences persist in terms of educational attainment and staying on rates post-16. Comprehensives have also failed to produce a meritocracy.
- There are significant differences in the pass rates of comprehensives depending on their catchment area. Schools in middle-class areas tend to have much higher pass rates than those in predominantly working-class areas.
- The 1990s saw further attacks on state schooling by Ofsted along with the marketisation of education. Schools are now in competition with each other for pupils and ultimately for their own survival.

Responses to the criticisms

- Educational pass rates have risen significantly between the 1960s and 1980s and today many more children leave school with qualifications than did in the tripartite system.
- Evidence suggests that children of the highest academic ability do as well in comprehensives as in other types of school.
- The state system has always had to compete with private schools and grammar schools. In many areas, private and grammar schools have 'creamed off' the brightest children, while the assisted-places scheme introduced by the Conservatives in 1980 allowed less affluent 'gifted' children to attend a private school without having to pay the fees.

1988 Education Reform Act

The 1988 Education Reform Act has had the most significant impact on schooling since 1944. It introduced a set of far-reaching reforms on education.

National Curriculum

For the first time in Britain the government decided which subjects should be studied in all state schools. English, maths and science became core subjects for all 11- to 16-year-olds and it also became compulsory for all secondary school students to study a foreign language.

Parental choice

The act encouraged parents to choose a secondary school for their child. Critics argue that, in reality, this choice only increased the social divisions in schools and allowed middle-class parents to play the system to their advantage.

National testing

With the aim of raising national standards, testing and national attainment targets were introduced for children at ages 7, 11, 14 and 16.

City technology colleges

These were inner-city schools that specialised in technology and were partly funded by the private sector. They were independent of the LEA.

Local management of schools (LMS)

The Act changed the nature of funding for schools. LMS meant that each school had more power over its budget. The responsibility for managing the budget was removed from the LEA and given to the head teacher and the governors.

Vocationalism

Vocationalism is the link between education and the labour market. It is the belief that education should be the training ground for employment and is often associated with ideas of the New Right. It is argued that education and training should help to promote economic growth by teaching the skills needed by the workforce. In the 1980s, a 'new vocationalism' developed under the Conservative governments led by Margaret Thatcher, during which a number of new measures were introduced.

- The Technical and Vocational Education Initiative (TVEI) was introduced in 1983 and extended nationally for all 14- to 18-year-old students. It broadened the curriculum and emphasised the importance of work experience for all.

- The Certificate of Pre-Vocational Education (CPVE) was introduced in 1985. Less academically able students were taught practical skills in order to prepare them for employment.
- National Vocational Qualifications and General National Vocational Qualifications (NVQs and GNVQs), introduced in 1993, remain on the curriculum and include leisure and tourism, business, information technology, health and social care.
- Training and Enterprise Councils (TECs) began in 1990 and are led by local business people who receive money for skills training to meet local needs. However, there is controversy over their efficacy.
- Youth Training Schemes (YTS) were designed for school leavers as a form of employment training rather than work experience. Young people are given opportunities to gain qualifications. However, the following criticisms have been levelled at the schemes:
  - they are used to restrict potential union members
  - the trainees are a source of cheap labour
  - the trainees are not counted as unemployed even with no guarantee of work after the scheme
  - new workers are kept in 'suspended animation' until jobs become available
  - trainees are substitutes for full-time workers who would have to be paid more
  - trainees are potentially de-skilled by being taught 'behavioural etiquette' rather than transferable skills — in this way they have been prepared for dis-empowerment

New Labour and educational policy

Since 1997, the new Labour government has emphasised the links between education and work. Their recent policies have included:
- reduction of class sizes
- home–school contracts
- target setting
- inspection of schools, including naming and shaming 'failing schools' and direct intervention in such schools by government agencies
- setting up of the Learning and Skills Council to oversee post-16 education and training in order to improve standards
- setting up education action zones together with social exclusion units to tackle problems emerging from areas of high social deprivation
- the New Deal — to get the young unemployed and lone parents back to work

Evaluation
+ New Labour has retained New Right policies on inspection and parental choice.
- New Right would criticise them for limiting parental choice by abolishing grant-maintained status for schools.

- Liberals would criticise them for taking an overly economic perspective on education.
- Marxists would criticise them for not dealing with inequality of opportunity.
- From a social-democratic perspective, they have failed to abolish selection and have not dealt with setting and streaming.
- Tuition fees for higher education students affect the economically underprivileged more than they affect others.

Questions
&
Answers

This section of the guide provides you with six questions on the topic of **Education** in the style of the AQA unit test. The first five questions are followed by a grade-A candidate response. It is important to note that these are not 'model answers' — they do not represent the only, or even necessarily the best, way of answering these questions. It would be quite possible, particularly in the answers to (e) and (f), to take a different approach, or to use different material, or even to come to a different conclusion, and still gain very high marks. Rather, the answers represent a particular 'style': one that answers the question set and displays the appropriate skills, including using suitable concepts and studies, displaying a critical and evaluative awareness towards the material used, and presenting a logically structured argument. The questions also have a grade-C candidate answer that is basically on the right track but which fails, for various reasons, to score very high marks.

A sixth question is provided which is not accompanied by a student answer, but is left for you to write your own. Again, some pointers are given to help put you on the right track.

Examiner's comments

The candidate answers are accompanied by examiner's comments. These are preceded by the icon 🄴 and indicate where credit is due. For the grade-A answers, the examiner shows you what it is that enables the candidates to score so highly. Particular attention is given to the candidates' use of the examinable skills: knowledge and understanding, and analysis and evaluation. For the grade-C answers, the examiner points out areas for improvement, specific problems and common errors. You are also invited to rewrite the answer in order to gain higher marks, and some pointers are given to show you how you might do this.

Socialisation and inequality

Item A

At first sight, a National Curriculum appears to provide a more level pitch on which pupils of differing social backgrounds can play for the rewards of schooling. However, the lack of legal requirements on independent schools to apply it means there are still two pitches. Some 7% of all pupils, and a much higher percentage of secondary pupils, attend independent schools. Such schools have pupils with particular social characteristics associated with educational success. The schools' ability to tailor a curriculum to student needs, especially with a view to entry to Oxbridge and higher education, further adds to their already considerable advantages, for example better staff–pupil ratios (1 to 10.4 compared with 1 to 16.1 in other schools, according to Department for Education and Employment figures in 1993).

Source: Reid, I. (1996) 'Education and inequality', *Sociology Review*, Vol. 6, No. 2.

Item B

What children learn in school is not simply the subjects on the official curriculum. Some sociologists would argue that the hidden curriculum plays an even greater role in the socialisation of pupils. The messages and ideologies that are passed on through the hidden curriculum help to reproduce the very social relations of production on which a capitalist system can be maintained.

(a) **What is meant by the term 'independent school' (Item A)?** (2 marks)

(b) **Suggest *two* benefits that the National Curriculum introduced for pupils.** (4 marks)

(c) **Suggest *three* ways in which schools socialise pupils.** (6 marks)

(d) **Identify and briefly explain *two* criticisms Marxists might make of the socialisation process within schools.** (8 marks)

(e) **Examine the importance of school factors on pupils' educational success.** (20 marks)

(f) **Using evidence from Items A and B and elsewhere, assess the view that the education system can be seen as meritocratic.** (20 marks)

Total: 60 marks

■ ■ ■

Answer to question 1: grade-C candidate

(a) An independent school is a private school which is sometimes run by a religious organisation.

Ɛ This is acceptable, and gains full marks.

(b) GCSE exams for all and opting out for parents.

> There is confusion here and the answer scores no marks.

(c) Through the hidden curriculum, which means everything you learn at school that's not on the timetable, pupils learn punctuality, respect for teachers and the value of hard work.

> This is a good attempt at a difficult question. The candidate has only given one of three possible ways that schools socialise pupils and provided three examples of this particular way, scoring just 2 out of 6 marks.

(d) One criticism that Marxists would make of the socialisation process in schools is that it stops students from being creative. This is what Bowles and Gintis found in their study. The second criticism is that schools prepare pupils to be exploited in the workforce.

> The candidate has successfully identified two correct criticisms, but the second point has not been developed, losing 2 marks. Had the fact that schools encourage pupils to see capitalism as fair and right been added, then full marks would have been gained.

(e) For the purposes of this essay, school factors will mean interaction between teachers and pupils, labelling, self-fulfilling prophecy and anti-school subcultures.
Interactionists argue that teacher expectations and labelling play an important role in a pupil's success in education.

> This is a reasonable start. The candidate has defined what school factors mean to him or her. However, in being so prescriptive the candidate has narrowed down what is about to be discussed in the rest of the essay.

Hargreaves argued that teachers assess pupils from the moment that they meet them. They type pupils as lazy, good, bad, troublesome etc. These labels have a powerful effect because if a pupil is labelled as a troublemaker this will affect his or her self-esteem. The television programme *The Eye of the Storm* showed that when the teacher put collars on the pupils and treated them differently because of the colour of their eyes, their test results went down.

> This paragraph starts well with appropriate sociological evidence. The reference to the television programme is rather simplistic and does not draw out the implications of the experiment in sufficient detail.

Interactionists believe that people live up to their labels, which is a self-fulfilling prophecy, and some labels are harder to get rid of than others.

> Again, although the candidate does have some understanding of the process of the self-fulfilling prophecy, the paragraph needs more development.

Peer pressure in schools can also affect pupils' progress. Many pupils join anti-school subcultures. In one study the 'lads' were not interested in school at all and

THE HENLEY COLLEGE LIBRARY

they were more interested in 'having a laff' and making fun of the boys who were hard working. The researcher argued that this was the way working-class boys got working-class jobs.

> ✒ This is a useful, if brief, reference to peer-group pressure, with some implicit reference to Willis's study.

So school factors are very important in the success of pupils. 'What teachers believe, their students achieve'. There are other processes too, like streaming and setting, which affect students.

> ✒ The essay comes to a rather abrupt end. This might have been an opportunity to elaborate on streaming and setting to show how they affect achievement. The candidate also fails to take into account the effect of the school ethos, using the results of the study undertaken by Rutter.

> ✒ **Overall, a fair attempt at the question, but more development of the points would score a higher mark. The candidate scores 14 out of 20 marks.**

(f) Marxists and functionalists see the education system in very different ways. Functionalists like Parsons and Durkheim see education as meritocratic. This means that everyone has the same chance of succeeding in school. Education teaches the next generation the skills necessary for work. Functionalists believe that society must be kept stable and in balance and that education is important in helping society to achieve social order. They say that everyone must have shared norms and values in order for the system to work.

> ✒ This is a reasonable opening paragraph. There are links made between functionalism and the ideas of meritocracy, but the candidate fails to make explicit the processes within education that make this happen.

But Marxists disagree. They see education as a tool of the bourgeoisie to keep the working classes down. In school, children learn to be obedient and to respect teachers. The system isn't fair for working-class children because they fail, and as one sociologist said, 'school teaches working-class boys how to get working-class jobs'. The lads in his study did not try to succeed in school and formed their own deviant subculture.

Bowles and Gintis said that the school system corresponded to capitalism and children are exploited by teachers. Capitalism needs workers who have been brainwashed to accept the power of the bourgeoisie.

> ✒ This paragraph stands in juxtaposition to the first. There is some, very limited, evaluation present.

In conclusion, functionalists and Marxists disagree about the role of education. However, from my understanding most sociologists would reject the idea that education is fair for everyone because working-class children, especially boys, tend to underachieve in school.

📝 There is more evaluation here even though it is limited.

📝 **This essay uses potentially relevant material, which really needs to be developed to gain higher marks. The skills that need to be developed here are those of evaluation and analysis. The candidate scores 12 out of 20 marks.**

■ ■ ■

Answer to question 1: grade-A candidate

(a) An independent school is a fee-paying or private school. This also includes the top public schools.

📝 This is a good answer and gains both marks. The candidate might have given an example in place of the second sentence and this would also count.

(b) All students have to follow the same curriculum, so more girls continue to take science subjects.

If a student moves from one part of the country to another, they should be able to carry on with the same subjects without too much disruption.

📝 These are two sound responses, for full marks. Can you think of any other benefits?

(c) By encouraging hard work to prepare students for the world of work. By setting rules to make students obedient and cooperative workers.

📝 These two answers each get 2 marks, but the question asks for *three*, so 2 marks are lost.

(d) Two criticisms that Marxists might make are that schools prepare us for capitalist society and that they teach us to be passive and obedient to authority. By preparing us for capitalism we are socialised into the ideology of capitalism — competition, individualism, and even getting students to start up enterprise schemes in business studies. Secondly, the hidden curriculum makes us accept authority by its system of rules, discipline and sanctions and by requiring punctuality, etc.

📝 Here the candidate has identified several factors that are acceptable as Marxist criticisms. It is possible to see passivity and obedience as parts of the process of becoming workers for capitalism, and the student does introduce the hidden curriculum into the second point. This answer gains full marks.

(e) It goes without saying that school factors play a decisive role in the success or otherwise of school students. In the 1970s Michael Rutter argued that the ethos of the school was the key to educational success. During the 15 000 hours spent in school, high expectations of teachers, consistency and preparation for lessons all counted towards the achievement of the students. He argued that this was the case even where students' home backgrounds were different.

> This is an excellent start. It is well focused and provides relevant evidence to support the argument.

Interactionists focus on what actually happens in schools, in the classroom, between staff and students and among students themselves. For interactionists, what happens in the classroom is socially constructed — this means that the negotiation and interactions are created by the individuals themselves. Roles and expectations are not fixed but are constantly changing to meet new situations.

> Here there is evidence located in a theoretical context. The candidate demonstrates very good knowledge and understanding.

Hargreaves demonstrated through his research that teachers assess pupils from the moment they meet them. They do this through three stages — speculation, elaboration and stabilisation. By the final stage teachers believe that they 'know' the pupil well enough to label them as a success or failure. Interactionists have shown us that labels are 'sticky'. Once labelled, pupils find it very difficult to shake off the image. When labelled as troublemaker or failure, a self-fulfilling prophecy is likely to occur.

In *Pygmalion in the Classroom*, Rosenthal and Jacobson demonstrated the importance of teacher expectations for pupils' achievement. Even though there were ethical and methodological problems with their research, they showed how the self-fulfilling prophecy took place.

Another important study is Rist's research of a kindergarten class. The teacher had labelled her 5-year-olds by the end of the first week and this labelling lasted for their time through primary school. Pupils were labelled as bright or otherwise on the basis of appearance and how they spoke rather than their abilities, and their achievements rested on their assignment to different groups. Rist concluded that 'what teachers believe, their pupils achieve'. Finally, not all interactionists accept this deterministic view of labelling. Margaret Fuller's research on Black girls showed that they were able to resist the labels of their teachers and achieve despite them.

> These three paragraphs provide excellent evidence to support the interactionist approach. They are all relevant to the question as they relate school factors to educational performance. The candidate also introduces a very important critique of interactionism by challenging the potential determinism of the approach.

Having examined school factors and how they affect students' progress, it is important to say that external factors like home background, poverty, health, etc. will all play a part in this process. No student grows up in a social vacuum.

> This conclusion introduces us to the other factors that have a part to play in educational success.

> **Some of the points could have been developed in this final paragraph. However, there is sufficient here for the answer to be awarded 17 marks.**

(f) A meritocratic education system means that pupils achieve success on the basis of their own efforts and ability. This view sees education as a neutral filtering system in which the most talented and hard-working succeed.

> This is a good introduction. The candidate introduces the concept early with a clear definition.

This view is held by functionalists who believe that the education system performs an essential role in the selection of people into appropriate roles in the economy. Parsons and, later, Davis and Moore saw education as meritocratic. Individuals are not intellectually equal. Intelligence is genetic and the role of the education system is to select the most able for the most functionally important roles in society. Therefore, doctors and lawyers should be naturally more intelligent than cleaners and porters. Parsons argued that a meritocratic education system was essential in an achievement-oriented society. Unlike the particularistic values within the family, the education system is based on universalistic values.

> In this paragraph there is development of the acceptance of a meritocracy from the functionalist perspective. As yet, there is no evaluation of the position, but the candidate is demonstrating knowledge and understanding of the argument.

However, not all functionalists shared this view. Melvin Tumin said that Davis and Moore's work was too simplistic because there was no way of measuring the functional importance of particular jobs.

> This short paragraph gives us the in-house critique from other functionalists.

Marxists, on the other hand, reject the view that the education system is meritocratic. Althusser saw education as an ideological state apparatus that legitimises class inequality in society. Bowles and Gintis showed that there was a correspondence between the education system and the economy. The economy cast a long shadow over education. This suggests schools are moulded according to the needs of capitalism. Through the hidden curriculum children learn to be obedient and to respect authority. Relationships between teachers and students are said to mirror those of employers and employees.

> This paragraph is both evaluative and analytical. The candidate is challenging the functionalist viewpoint directly by using the Marxist critique.

Willis carried out an ethnographic study on 12 working-class boys in which he showed that the boys could see through the system even though it meant that they still ended up with working-class jobs. He argued that the education system prepared working-class kids for working-class jobs.

We can see from Item A that despite the National Curriculum, education is far from a level playing field, because there is still a system of private education and wealthy people can buy privilege for their children. Item A shows us that only 7% of all pupils attend an independent school but they are far more likely than state students to gain a place at Oxbridge. This was shown recently in the case of a comprehensive school student with four A grades at A-level who was refused a place at Oxbridge.

In conclusion we can see that the system is a long way from being meritocratic and the wealthier you are the more likely you are to succeed.

⟨e⟩ This paragraph makes good use of Item A to show that a pupil's background has an important part to play in success, thus challenging the meritocratic argument.

⟨e⟩ **This candidate demonstrates excellent sociological knowledge and understanding, and a sophisticated grasp of criticisms, scoring 19 marks.**

Selection and success

Item A

It seems clear that school selection will remain an important educational issue, regardless of which political party forms the government of this country. A divided secondary system, with its hierarchy of schools firmly established, will continue to work to the advantage of the powerful, the influential and the articulate; while large numbers of children find themselves in less-favoured institutions which attract the sort of criticisms once levelled at the secondary modern schools, struggling to acquire respectability in postwar Britain.

Source: adapted from Chitty, C. (1997) 'Choose...education?', *Sociology Review*, Vol. 6, No. 4.

Item B

A 16-year-old girl at a private school says, 'Private schools are different. They make you want different things, think in different ways...they produce completely different sorts of people from state schools.'

There are a number of factors that might help to explain the differences found between the private- and state-school girls in this research. They include:

- *the investment factor* — many of the private-school girls and their parents talked of private education in terms of an investment

- *the limited experience of many of the private-school pupils* — few of the private-school girls had any experience of such things as unemployment, poverty or less-able young people

- *the friendship groups of the girls* — the majority of the private-school girls were found to socialise exclusively with other girls from their school

- *the lack of ideological alternatives at the school* — there was little real political discussion at the private school...at the state school, the girls experienced a much wider range of political and social views

Source: adapted from Roker, D. (1994) 'Girls in private schools', *Sociology Review*, Vol. 4, No. 2.

(a) **Explain what is meant by a 'secondary modern school' (Item A).**　　　　(2 marks)

(b) **Suggest *two* reasons why 'a divided secondary system...will continue to work to the advantage of the powerful, the influential and the articulate' (Item A).**　　　　(4 marks)

(c) **Give *three* ways in which friendship groups might affect a pupil's school performance.**　　　　(6 marks)

(d) Identify and explain **two** reasons why both parents and schoolgirls saw private education as an investment (Item **B**). (8 marks)

(e) Explain how state policies have affected the education system since the 1980s. (20 marks)

(f) Using evidence from Items **A** and **B** and elsewhere, assess the claim that social class is the major factor affecting educational success. (20 marks)

Total: 60 marks

Answer to question 2: grade-C candidate

(a) A comprehensive school.

🖉 This is incorrect — 0 marks.

(b) Firstly, middle-class parents have more money and therefore can afford to pay for their children's education. Secondly, middle-class pupils tend to be in the higher streams of comprehensives.

🖉 The candidate has identified two brief, but correct, reasons in answer to the question and gains full marks.

(c) In Willis's study the 'lads' formed an anti-school subculture that rejected teachers and the school. They were only interested in having a 'laff' and getting a job. The 'ear'oles' were more interested in getting qualifications. If you were being bullied you would probably stop going to school because you were afraid.

🖉 The first point about Willis's study is correct and scores 2 marks. However, the point about the ear'oles is not a direct answer to the question and gains no marks. The candidate has lost focus. The final statement does not relate to friendship groups and therefore does not score.

(d) The parents believed that spending their money on their daughters' education would get them better exam grades and more chance of going to university.

🖉 This is a correct response, but the candidate has only given one of the required two reasons and therefore scores only half marks.

(e) There have been many changes to the education system since the 1980s. Firstly, there was the tripartite system. This meant that children had to take the 11-plus exam in order to decide which secondary school they attended. This test was an IQ test and many sociologists feel that this was unfair because middle-class children were much better prepared for these tests than working-class children. We also know that if you practise these tests then you will improve your score.

🖉 Unfortunately, the candidate has not read the question carefully enough and has not written about the correct historical period. Although the knowledge is correct, it is not focused on the question.

question

The National Curriculum was introduced in 1988 as part of the Education Reform Act. This brought about a common curriculum for all students. All students have to study English, maths and science until they are 16. It also introduced national tests for all 7-, 11- and 14-year-olds. Now girls cannot give up science at 13 like many of them used to. The government also introduced league tables in the 1980s which mean that schools are now in competition with each other. Each school has to publish its GCSE results so that parents can see how successful it has been.

> The essay is now coming into focus as the candidate is examining some of the key changes to education in the 1980s.

GCSEs were also introduced in the 1980s and coursework became a key part of most GCSE courses. Girls started to achieve more passes in school than boys. Some sociologists argued that this was because girls work more consistently than boys.

> Again the material is relevant to the question, and the candidate ties this in with gender changes in educational achievement. However, the paragraph would have been improved if the candidate had demonstrated the links within the material more clearly.

Finally, the other policy that the government introduced was called 'new vocationalism'. This linked school with the world of work. The New Right believed that it was very important for all students to be prepared for the workplace. They introduced work experience and National Records of Achievement so that students, on leaving school, could show potential employers their achievements.

However, Marxists would say that new vocationalism is just another way of keeping the working class in their place by preparing them for working-class jobs.

> A fairly balanced argument which draws from two relevant perspectives.

> **This answer shows sound knowledge and understanding and some limited AO2 skills. To increase the score a balanced conclusion should have been added — the candidate has left the conclusion to be drawn by the reader. The essay scores 14 marks.**

(f) Sociologists argue that working-class children tend to do less well in school for a number of reasons. Firstly, children might live in poverty. This would mean having no money to buy books and no chance to have a computer at home. They may live in overcrowded and damp housing which would cause illness and they would have to have more time off school.

> This is a sound introductory paragraph which focuses on material deprivation.

Douglas argued that working-class parents take less interest in their children's education whereas middle-class parents are much more concerned that their children stay on in school, and they attend parents' evenings much more frequently. However, Douglas can be criticised because he did not take into account that it is much harder for working-class parents to attend the school if they do shift work.

Middle-class and upper-class parents have the option of going private if there is not a school they like in the area. They have the money to be able to buy the best for their children and we know that if you go to a public school then you are much more likely to attend a top university afterwards.

 There is some useful material in this section. The candidate has provided evidence from sociological research to show the differences between the social classes. However, so far it is assumed that all working-class students underachieve and all middle-class students are successful.

Bernstein said that working-class and middle-class children used different language codes. Working-class children normally spoke with the restricted code, a type of slang which uses short sentences. Middle-class children used the elaborated code — this is the language of the school and it is much more formal. Middle-class children are therefore at an advantage because they speak and write in the same way as the teachers.

 There is relevant material here, even though it is dated. There is some limited evidence of AO2 skills.

In conclusion, it is clear that the higher up the social class scale you are, the better you will do in education. However, it is important to remember that social class is not the only factor that affects children's attainment. Factors such as gender and ethnicity are important too.

 Some evaluation is evident in the conclusion. However, the candidate does not address the other factors that could be equally important to social class, such as gender, ethnicity, neighbourhood and the school itself.

 Overall, this is a reasonable sociological essay, and is awarded 13 marks.

■ ■ ■

Answer to question 2: grade-A candidate

(a) Under the tripartite system, pupils went to this type of school if they had 'failed' the 11-plus exam.

 This is a good response that places the school within the context of the tripartite system. It gains both marks.

(b) Middle-class parents are more likely to understand the education system as they have more personal experience of it. They could even pay to get their children into private grammar schools.

Middle-class pupils will have more cultural capital and will be more likely to get grammar school places.

question

🖉 A good response, for full marks. It includes more than two points but they are all well explained.

(c) Friends may influence you to join anti-school subcultures.

Competition among friends to be high achievers might improve a student's grades.

Fuller found that Black girls formed a group that worked together to resist negative labelling and they were therefore successful.

🖉 Three clear and accurate responses given — anti-school subcultures, competition and resistance — for all **6 marks.**

(d) Private schools get better exam results and so parents are prepared to pay for what they think is a better education for their children.

Cultural capital becomes economic capital — parents believe that their girls will get better opportunities in the labour market.

🖉 Two correct responses clearly identified and explained, for full marks.

(e) There have been many changes to the education system since the 1980s. The Conservative government or the New Right wanted to make education more work-orientated and make students more prepared to fit the needs of industry. This was done in several ways.

🖉 This is a good introduction and well focused on the question. The candidate has already introduced the idea of theory into the answer.

Firstly, the government introduced the idea of GNVQ. These are vocational qualifications which are designed to encourage students to be more focused on the needs of industry and better prepared for their future careers. Students who are generally seen as less academic are encouraged to study for GNVQ rather than the gold standard of A-level, but even here a recent change in the form of Curriculum 2000 has split the A-level course into two separate courses with an AS qualification at the end of the first year. Students are now encouraged to gain key skills qualifications in post-16 education.

🖉 Again we see that this candidate is well informed on recent changes in the education system and is connecting these to the needs of the economy.

All year 10 pupils have to do work experience and in many schools year 12 students attend work experience too. All students have to produce a National Record of Achievement document at the end of year 11, which is designed to act as a CV for future employers. Bowles and Gintis would argue that this is serving the interests of capitalism because students are simply being brainwashed into accepting capitalism as natural and normal.

🖉 This paragraph is making specific reference to Marxist theory and linking education to the needs of a capitalist society.

The 1988 Education Reform Act changed the education system in a radical way. It introduced the National Curriculum and all students now follow the same curriculum in England and Wales from age 5 to 16 in the core subjects of English, maths and science. Children are tested throughout their school careers as well. Pupils have to sit SATs and the levels achieved by schools are made public.

Although this paragraph would be better earlier in the essay, it makes relevant points and is focused on recent changes.

In conclusion we can see that the many changes that have taken place seem to link education with the needs of the world of work. Although the functionalists would see this as a necessary part of the role of the education system, Marxists see it as more sinister, as a means of perpetuating the class system.

This paragraph concludes the essay and brings in two theories on education. However, the comment on Marxists is not focused specifically on the question.

A very sound response, deserving 18 marks.

(f) According to Item A, 'a divided secondary system...will continue to work to the advantage of the powerful, the influential and the articulate'. This means that the school system benefits children from middle- and upper-class backgrounds. Therefore, social class is still a very important factor in the success of some groups of children.

This in an excellent start. The candidate has used Item A effectively and is focused on the question. It is good to see that in the first paragraph there is some evidence of evaluation.

It has long been argued by sociologists that coming from a working-class background disadvantages some children. There are many studies that support this view. Douglas found that material deprivation disadvantaged some working-class children but the key factor in affecting educational success was parental interest. He said that middle-class parents showed more interest in their children's education by visiting the school on more occasions than working-class parents. However, he did not take into account that many working-class parents worked shifts and therefore could not attend parents' evenings.

Here the candidate has successfully applied a relevant study to meet the criteria of the question, and the material has also been evaluated.

Cultural deficit theorists such as Sugarman and Hyman have placed the blame for working-class underachievement on the working-class culture. They argue that working-class parents socialise their children differently and encourage them to leave school at the first opportunity. For them there is a culture clash between the home and the school. However, these studies are very dated now and many sociologists would reject this view. They ignored issues of poverty and the effect of the school on achievement. Interactionists such as Becker have argued that teachers prefer to teach middle-class pupils. They are seen to be much closer to the ideal. Middle-class pupils are also much more likely to be placed in higher streams in school than working-class pupils.

This is a well-balanced paragraph containing relevant sociological material. The candidate uses sociological studies to good effect and remains focused on the question.

Other theorists also argue that social class is the major factor affecting educational success. The Marxist sociologist Boudon argued that inequality in education is inevitable because we live in a class-based society. Middle-class students need to go to university to maintain their class position but a working-class student who goes to university may leave their family and friends behind. Bourdieu argued that middle-class pupils succeed in school because they have cultural capital. Their accent and manners give them advantages in school.

In conclusion, having examined the evidence, it is clear that social class is still a major factor affecting educational attainment. However, it is important to remember that gender and ethnicity also play a part. Rutter said that despite social class, schools make a real difference to the success or failure of pupils. Finally, the postmodernists would argue that class is less important than it used to be.

A good evaluative conclusion that relates back to the question, but which also raises other factors that might be as important as social class. Although the comment about the postmodernists seems like an afterthought, it is nevertheless a relevant point.

This is a sound, well-argued essay which stays focused on the question. It demonstrates all the relevant skill domains and the answer is clearly structured, giving it 18 marks out of 20.

Gender and social class

Item A

There are marked differences between the sexes in education. Until the late 1980s, the major concern was with the underachievement of girls. However, in the early 1990s girls began to outperform boys in all areas and at all levels of the education system. The main problem today is with the underachievement of boys...there are also concerns that girls could do even better if teachers spent as much time with girls as they are forced to do with boys. (As a result, many people argue that pupils should be educated in single-sex institutions.)

Source: adapted from Mitsos, E. and Browne, K. (1998) 'Gender differences in education', *Sociology Review*, Vol. 8, No. 1.

Item B

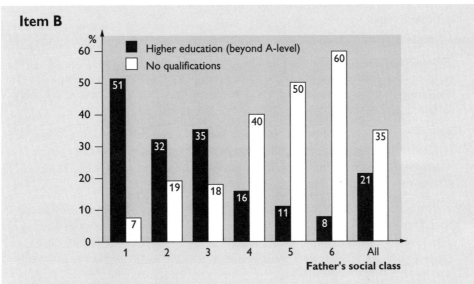

Figure 1 Percentage of persons with higher or no educational qualifications, by father's social class, Great Britain (1990–91)

Source: *General Household Survey*, 1991

(a) **What does 'single-sex' education mean?** (2 marks)

(b) **Identify and briefly describe *two* trends apparent in Figure 1.** (4 marks)

(c) **Suggest *three* ways in which boys and girls are treated differently in schools.** (6 marks)

(d) **Identify and explain *two* ways in which the father's social class position could affect a child's educational achievement.** (8 marks)

(e) **Examine the differences between Marxist and functionalist approaches to the relationship between education and the economy.** (20 marks)

(f) **Using evidence from Items A and B and elsewhere, assess competing sociological explanations for recent gender differences in educational achievement.** (20 marks)

Total: 60 marks

Answer to question 3: grade-C candidate

(a) Single-sex education means educating girls and boys separately, usually in different schools.

> 🖉 This is a correct response, for full marks.

(b) The lower your father's social class the more likely you are to have no qualifications.

> 🖉 The candidate has correctly identified one trend but failed to identify two and so loses 2 marks.

(c) Teachers tend to give boys more attention in the classroom. Spender found that boys dominate the classroom and girls are invisible. Boys do metalwork and girls do cooking. Careers teachers still tend to give different advice. For example, boys are rarely encouraged to study for NNEB courses but childcare courses are seen as normal for girls.

> 🖉 The candidate has successfully identified two ways in which boys and girls are treated differently: teachers giving boys more attention, and gendered careers advice. However, the statement about gender and subjects is about choice, not treatment, and so the answer loses 2 marks.

(d) If your father is poor or unskilled then you may have poorer home circumstances. Your home may be damp and you could get a lot of chest infections as a result. This would mean that you missed a lot of school through illness. If your father is upper class then you would almost certainly attend a public school like Eton or Harrow.

> 🖉 Here the candidate has presented two correct ways in which a father's social class could affect a child's educational achievement. In the first case the candidate has identified and explained the relationship, for all 4 marks. However, the second example gains only half marks because there is no adequate explanation of the link between upper-class fathers and attendance at public schools.

(e) Functionalists believe that society is harmonious and all parts of society, like education and the family, work together for the good of society. Parsons argued that education was a bridge between home and school where at home children are treated as family members while in school they are judged on their achievement. So education prepares children for wider society.

🖉 A reasonable introduction, although there is no link between functionalism and the wider society until the last sentence, and there is no reference to the economy.

In school, pupils learn norms and values that are necessary for work, like the values of hard work for instance. Other functionalists have said that school sorts the most able into the most important positions in society — like doctors and lawyers — while the less able become cleaners and factory workers.

🖉 This paragraph does make the link between school and the economy, but there is little development. There is no analysis or explanation of the ways in which school 'sorts' people into these positions. There is no critique of the determinism of this argument.

Marxists, however, see education in a different way. They believe that it works only in the interests of the ruling class and capitalism. Working-class pupils are sorted into working-class jobs through learning obedience, exploitation and other things in the hidden curriculum. Bowles and Gintis said that education reproduced the labour force. It was not a meritocracy. Willis said that education taught working-class boys to stay working class.

🖉 Here we have juxtaposition of the Marxist argument and there is some sociological evidence cited. Again, we would hope to see more development of the arguments. What other evidence would you use here?

So both functionalists and Marxists see schools as preparing students for the world of work, but functionalists see it as benefiting all of society, not just the ruling class.

🖉 This conclusion adds very little to the answer.

🖉 **This essay is brief but correctly focused and uses potentially relevant material which would need developing to increase the mark. It is awarded 13 out of 20 marks.**

(f) Item A says that girls should be educated in single-sex schools. According to some feminists, like Spender and Stanworth, girls' underachievement in education is down to what happens to them in the classroom. Teachers spend a lot more time with boys and some don't even know the girls' names. Teachers have lower expectations of girls' careers and so girls are less confident in school.

🖉 Although the candidate has not understood Item A clearly, this is a fair introduction to the essay.

However, girls have recently shown themselves to be more successful than boys, achieving more and higher GCSE passes, and the government has become more worried about what is going to happen to the boys.
  These are some reasons why girls are more successful:
• the introduction of coursework since the 1980s has helped girls achieve higher grades as they work more over the year

question

- the independence of women has shown girls that they can look after them-selves — girls are more career-minded now than in the 1970s
- the National Curriculum means that boys and girls have to study core subjects like science and maths and so girls have not been able to drop science, and have done well at it
- parents' attitudes have changed to encouraging their daughters to do well, not just to get married

So we can see that all these things work together to put girls ahead of boys.

This demonstrates relevant knowledge and understanding. However, displaying the material in bullet-points like this prevents analysis and evaluation of the points made. We recommend that you do this only if you are very short of time in an examination. However, running out of time is an indication of poor time management on the other questions and should be avoided.

The material in the essay is all potentially relevant and would be marked as such, but lack of analysis and evaluation reduces the mark to 9 out of 20.

Answer to question 3: grade-A candidate

(a) Single-sex education means a system where schools are attended by only girls or boys. It usually refers to secondary schools, but primary schools can also be single-sex.

This is a correct response and gains full marks.

(b) The higher the social class position of their fathers, the lower is the chance of people gaining no qualifications. The lower the social class of fathers the lower is the likelihood of higher qualifications for their children.

These are accurate trends identified from Item B and score full marks.

(c) Teacher expectations — boys are seen as disruptive and girls as good pupils. Career advice/subject choices — these are gendered and often stereotyped. Sport — sports are often divided so that boys cannot take netball and girls cannot take rugby.

Three correct responses have been identified and explained, gaining full marks. Can you think of any others?

(d) One way in which a father's social class can affect his child's educational devel-opment is by being middle-class, as children of middle-class parents have more cultural capital than working-class children and this gives them a headstart in school. Also, if your father is an unskilled manual worker you have a much poorer chance of getting to university and you are more likely to leave school at 16.

Two correct responses which are clearly focused on the consequences of social class on education. Again, full marks are scored.

(e) As macro-perspectives, both functionalism and Marxism examine education as part of the social structure. They see it performing important functions for the economy, but their explanations are very different.

2 This is a well-focused opening paragraph.

The functionalist approach, starting with Durkheim, saw education as a force for social solidarity by transmitting shared social norms and values to the next generation. Parsons continued this approach by arguing that education performed a vital role in bridging the gap between the family, based on particularistic values and the economy, based on universalistic values.

2 The candidate is demonstrating very good knowledge and understanding and is keeping to the theme of education and the economy.

Davis and Moore paid particular attention to the selection function of education by arguing that it was only education which was able to sift and sort the most talented individuals into the functionally most important positions in society. However, these assumptions have been questioned by other sociologists, in terms of what makes one job functionally more important than another. This was seen recently in the fuel crisis of September 2000 when many professional jobs were affected by the action of lorry drivers. It showed that we are all inter-dependent.

2 This is a useful paragraph, developing the functionalist position, and including evaluation and identification of a contemporary example.

On the other hand, Marxists are much more critical of the role of education in the economy. They argue that education merely serves to reproduce a willing and obedient workforce for the capitalist system. Bowles and Gintis claimed that the economy 'cast a long shadow' over education. The social relations between employer and employee are mirrored by the social relations between teachers and pupils in schools. For Bowles and Gintis, the hidden curriculum performed a vital function in reproducing the next labour force with the appropriate attitudes.

2 This paragraph criticises the functionalists and uses evidence in an entirely appropriate way.

In conclusion, both perspectives examine education from a structuralist perspective. Both clearly identify a relationship between the education system and the economy. However, for the functionalists this is to the benefit of the whole system, whereas for the Marxists it benefits the capitalists.

2 In this conclusion the candidate compares the two perspectives, finding both similarities and differences.

2 **This is a sophisticated response deserving 18 marks.**

(f) As Item A says, there are marked differences between the sexes in education. Earlier the concern was with the underachievement of girls and now it has switched to that of boys. Statistics of examination results show that since 1975 girls have outstretched boys when it comes to attainment. However, the most dramatic improvements have been since around 1987 when, although boys and girls improved their scores at GCSE, girls went even further ahead.

> The candidate makes use of the item from the introductory sentence. There is a pleasing blend of evaluation, knowledge and understanding here.

A *Panorama* documentary called 'The future is female' revealed how boys were underachieving right from primary school. It argued that parental attitudes had changed and parents were now putting more emphasis on their daughters' education. Parents were more likely to read to their daughters and to take time listening to them reading. They also had higher expectations of the girls throughout their school lives. This would be one possible reason why girls are doing better. However, Tanya Hope criticised the documentary, claiming that the boys were not underachieving but had actually increased their scores over the past 10 years. Therefore, perhaps it is not the changing nature of boys that we should be examining but that of girls.

> Relevant media material is used here but not uncritically. It is important that students make use of relevant, contemporary media material, but see it as a mediated product, which should therefore be treated carefully.

Harvey Goldstein showed that girls did better than boys even with the 11-plus examination, but LEAs marked them down so that there were more even numbers of girls and boys going to grammar schools. This may be an indication that girls have not suddenly outperformed boys in education, but that overall factors in wider society, including biased attitudes towards women, have simply dampened their performance in the past. Sue Sharpe, in a study in the 1980s, seems to agree with this. She claimed that girls placed little emphasis on educational success. However, this might have been partly a result of lack of encouragement from parents and teachers because when she revisited the study a decade later she found that girls had changed their attitudes to educational achievement.

> This paragraph calls on more supportive evidence to substantiate the argument that the performance of girls over that of boys may not be a new phenomenon.

The studies of Stanworth, Deem and Spender all pointed to differential treatment of girls in the classroom. However, since the early 1980s, the new developments in education like GIST and WISE and the introduction of TVEI all encouraged girls to widen their horizons. It may be that the new focus on equal opportunities actually left some of the boys behind.

However, there is some evidence that the changes brought by the National Curriculum encouraged greater achievement of girls. Since they have had to study science and maths, which were traditionally seen as 'male' areas, they have shown how successful they can be here too. Sociological explanations vary concerning the changes in gender achievement. However, the main suggestions seem to centre on feminist ideas having raised awareness and thus encouraged girls in school and in the labour market.

📝 These two paragraphs examine the contemporary evidence together with sociological explanations for the differences.

More recently, some sociologists have focused on the underachievement of boys and have pointed to a potential 'crisis of masculinity'. There are several factors that might affect the progress of boys and they include: a decline in manual industries and skilled manual occupations; a rise in unemployment for men; changes in families which may have created more 'absentee fathers'; the rise of a 'laddish' culture, especially with some young men's magazines and some television programmes like *Men Behaving Badly*.

However, the postmodernists would argue that gender identities have become more fragmented so that there is less emphasis on gender stereotyping and gender expectations in education.

📝 This is an excellent answer and probably beyond the capability of many students in examination conditions. However, some candidates can produce responses as sophisticated as this and are rewarded at the highest level. This answer gains full marks.

uestion 4

Achievement and ethnicity

Item A

Recent research shows some of the complexities of the arguments about racism in schools. The Black Child Report (1997), produced by Amenta Marketing, which specialises in researching lifestyles and attitudes among the ethnic minority communities in the UK, carries interviews with 374 children of African and African-Caribbean descent, aged between 11 and 16 years, at schools in London, Birmingham, Manchester, Liverpool, Nottingham and Bristol.

Twenty-two percent of the sample reported racism by a teacher in the previous month and 15% claimed to have suffered racism from pupils during the same period. Also, 38% are reported to have liked the idea of attending a Black-only school.

Source: adapted from Pilkington, A. (1990) 'Are schools racist?', *Sociology Review*, Vol. 8, No. 3.

Item B

Sociologists who take an interactionist perspective examine the processes within schools rather than the relationship of the education system to the wider social structure. These processes, such as labelling, self-fulfilling prophecy and negotiations between staff and students, play a crucial role in creating children as pupils who are more or less successful within the system. The poorer educational achievement of working-class children and Afro-Caribbean boys is seen as a product of the processes of interaction and negotiation which go on between these pupils and their teachers.

(a) **What does 'self-fulfilling prophecy' mean? (Item B)** (2 marks)

(b) **Identify and briefly describe *two* examples of teacher–pupil interaction which might affect pupil performance.** (4 marks)

(c) **Suggest *three* ways in which the methodology of the research reported in Item A might be criticised.** (6 marks)

(d) **Identify and explain *two* ways in which the British education system might be seen as ethnocentric.** (8 marks)

(e) **Examine competing sociological explanations of the role of vocational education.** (20 marks)

(f) **Using evidence from Items A and B and elsewhere, critically discuss the reasons for the relative underachievement of ethnic minority pupils in Britain today.** (20 marks)

Total: 60 marks

Answer to question 4: grade-C candidate

(a) Self-fulfilling prophecy means someone lives up to the label.

> Although the candidate has some vague idea of the concept, this answer is insufficient and gains no marks.

(b) Some teachers label pupils as 'hopeless', and therefore the student does not try to achieve.

Some teachers are racist and treat Black boys as troublemakers. The boys then become disruptive in class and may form anti-school subcultures.

> The candidate has correctly identified two reasons and gains full marks.

(c) The survey says that 38% wanted a Black-only school. We can criticise this idea because it will not help race relations.

> The candidate has misunderstood the question, which asks for criticism of the methodology and not the findings. The answer therefore gains no marks.

(d) Ethnocentrism means to view one's own culture as superior to others. Firstly, the British education system can be seen to be racist because there are very few Black and Asian head teachers. Secondly, in English literature, you don't get to read any Black or Asian authors.

> The candidate has successfully identified two correct responses, for **8 marks**.

(e) The term vocational education means education that is related to the world of work. This includes work experience in school, vocational courses like GNVQs and training courses such as the YTS and New Deal. Vocational education started in Britain in the 1980s when the New Right became very concerned that students were not properly prepared for industry. They believed that it was essential that all pupils learned about the world of work while they were still in school. According to the New Right, unemployment is caused by the lack of skilled young people; it is not an economic problem.

> This is a very good introduction. The candidate defines the concept and links it to political intervention into education.

Functionalists would argue that vocational education is very important because they see education as a filtering system and the most talented and intelligent should get the most functionally important roles in society. Vocational education will prepare pupils for fitting into society better. However, Marxists disagree. Bowles and Gintis said that work casts a long shadow over the education system and the real purpose of school is to reproduce the next generation of workers for capitalism. They see schemes like the YTS as simply a way to keep young people off the unemployment register and to give companies cheap labour. Some sociologists believe that YTS members are neither real students nor real workers because they do not get proper wages.

question

 This is another good paragraph. It shows clear understanding of the Marxist approach to vocational education. The candidate has a sound grasp of the view that this form of education is a manipulation of young people.

 This essay is rather unbalanced. Although it does pay some regard to functionalist views, it has not really addressed the more positive aspects of vocational education. However, there is some evidence of knowledge and understanding of the Marxist approach to the subject. 13 marks are awarded.

(f) In general, ethnic minority pupils do tend to underachieve in school. There are several reasons that sociologists put forward to explain this underachievement. Firstly, schools and teachers have been accused of being racist.

 Many candidates assume that ethnic minorities all underachieve. It appears this candidate is going to do this.

Bernard Coard said that the British education system made the Black child educationally subnormal. Teachers treat Black boys as troublemakers and often see them as aggressive and as a threat in the classroom. Jayleigh School is an example of a school that was racist. In the school, streaming was closely linked to race. Asian students were placed in lower streams and so they were not entered for as many GCSEs as White students. Since this study, Jayleigh has changed its attitudes.

 Here the candidate has differentiated between students, if only implicitly, by examining the position of Black boys and Asian pupils.

According to Cecile Wright, ethnic minority pupils in primary school were treated differently from White pupils. Asian pupils were ignored by teachers who thought that they could not speak English. Black boys were treated unfairly. They were expected to behave badly and were punished by the teacher. Black pupils are much more likely to be permanently excluded from school compared with White pupils. This is due to the racism of many teachers. Other sociologists have seen language and home background as important factors and, as Item A says, some Black parents have set up Black-only schools.

 There is some reasonable material here and the candidate also makes reference to the item.

 The essay lacks a conclusion, but overall it is focused on the question and the material is relevant. It scores 12 out of 20 marks.

■ ■ ■

Answer to question 4: grade-A candidate

(a) Self-fulfilling prophecy means the labelling of someone by someone else in power and the person living up to that label. The label is usually negative but it can be a positive label too.

📝 This is a full response, which gains the 2 marks. (It would gain 2 marks for the first sentence alone.)

(b) Fuller found that a group of Afro-Caribbean girls resisted the negative label of their teacher and worked against expectations.

Rosenthal and Jacobson found that the 'spurters' actually achieved higher scores at the end of the year, so they assumed teacher expectations had worked.

📝 These are correctly identified and described, for full marks.

(c) The research could be criticised for the following reasons:
- the sample size is small (only 374 children) so the data may not be representative
- there are no Asian or Chinese children even though it is supposed to be about ethnic minorities
- it does not say where the interviews were carried out and it might have made a difference if they were done in schools

📝 Three correct responses, gaining all 6 marks. How many more could you find?

(d) The British education system could be seen as ethnocentric because:
- the curriculum could be biased towards White culture, especially in history
- languages — those taught are usually European and not Asian or African
- staffing — there is often a lack of Black teachers, but cleaners and caretakers may be Black

📝 These three responses are correct and clearly identified. However, only two are needed for full marks.

(e) Although new vocationalism has most closely been identified with New Right thinking and the policies of the Conservative Party of the 1980s and 1990s, the introduction of new vocationalism in education can clearly be pinpointed to the 'Ruskin speech' of 1976 made by the then Labour Prime Minister James Callaghan. He argued that Britain's decline in manufacturing and rising unemployment was caused in part by schools failing to produce young people who had the right skills and attitudes for industry. This speech was extremely influential among policy-makers and led to a 'revolution' in schools in the 1980s. For the first time since the Second World War, education was explicitly connected to the world of work.

📝 This is an extremely good introductory paragraph. The candidate has located new vocationalism in a historical context and made the connection between education and work. Other candidates might have defined the concept in this paragraph, but it is obvious here that the idea of 'new vocationalism' is clearly understood.

The New Right took on the mantle of educational reform in the 1980s with the Education Reform Act of 1988, the single biggest reform to schooling since the 1944 Butler Act. The Tories introduced a National Curriculum for all state pupils, testing at key stages, and the publication of league tables which were meant to encourage competition and introduce market forces to make schools more business-like and efficient. The New Right believed that all pupils needed to gain work experience so that they were fully prepared for their futures. All year 10 pupils now have to undergo a period of work experience, as do many year 12 students. NRAs are also compulsory for all school leavers. These are records of pupil achievement for future employers.

> *Again this is a very sound paragraph. The evidence on educational reform is linked to the question and the paragraph is well focused throughout.*

One of the biggest changes to schools has been the introduction of GNVQs. These are vocational courses in subject areas including travel and tourism, business, and health and social care. GNVQs are offered at three levels. These are foundation, intermediate and advanced, the latter being equivalent to two A-levels. According to the New Right, GNVQs will prepare students better for the world of work, equipping them with transferable skills needed by industry. However, critics such as Cohen have questioned the notion of transferable skills, arguing that this is nothing more than learning the right attitude for work. Marxists argue that the hidden curriculum of training schemes and GNVQ courses teaches students to accept capitalism as natural and normal, and the courses are really designed to reduce the unemployment statistics. According to Braverman, education has become a baby-sitting service for adolescents. Many sociologists would assert that there is a clear relationship between class and vocational courses. Middle-class parents still view A-levels as the gold standard of education and do not want their children to study for GNVQs.

> *This paragraph displays all the skills necessary for an AS answer. There is very good knowledge and understanding and a pleasing evaluative tone to the arguments.*

Marxist writers are very critical of the role of training schemes for young people because they claim that the emphasis is one that blames the individual for unemployment and does not identify the economy as the cause. Dan Finn argued that the training schemes of the 1980s encouraged the working class to know their place and become an easily exploitable workforce. He also claimed that YTS schemes and now the New Deal are simply ways of giving free labour to employers.

> *Here the candidate develops the argument from the Marxist perspective, providing evidence to substantiate the position.*

In conclusion, it is clear from this discussion that new vocationalism has been an important feature of educational policy since the 1980s. It has been strongly advocated by the New Right as the way forward in schools but is strongly resisted by the left as a way of brainwashing the working class.

> *This paragraph is essential in bringing the essay to a reasoned conclusion and gains more AO2 skill marks.*

This is an exceptionally good answer. The candidate demonstrates a sophis-ticated understanding and has structured the essay very well. It is probably much longer than could be produced within the time constraints of the examination. However, it is reproduced here to show you what might be possible. The answer gains full marks.

(f) Item B suggests that through interaction between teachers and pupils, some ethnic minority students achieve less than other groups in education. Various explana-tions have been put forward for such ethnic minority underachievement, and thus the reasons why these students may face discrimination within the education system.

The candidate uses material from Item B in the introductory paragraph and introduces some analysis early in the essay. This is always a good thing. It is much better to demonstrate the skills as you progress through the essay rather than waiting until the conclusion to produce your evaluation.

Firstly, language barriers may present a problem for some students, especially where English is not their mother tongue and where it is not used as the main language at home. However, Ballard and Driver argue that such problems cease to exist by the time the student reaches 16, claiming that students of this age are as fluent in English as their classmates.

Family life may also present problems for achievement. Ken Pryce suggests that Afro-Caribbean families are 'turbulent', lacking a 'sense of close dependence on each other'. Indeed, the view is that these families often fail to provide adequate cultural capital for their children. The higher proportion of lone-parent families within this group is seen by some commentators as another reason for their relative failure.

Both of these paragraphs provide very useful material relevant to the argument that underachievement in education is related to home factors. This should now be balanced by evidence of in-school factors.

However, the Swann Report challenged many of these stereotypical views and indicated that if class were not a factor, these students would not be disadvan-taged. Indeed, the report claimed that low social class accounted for at least 80% of educational underachievement. Social class is more significant for specific ethnic minority groups, such as those from Bangladesh and Pakistan and some Afro-Caribbean students, as these groups are disproportionately working class.

Bernard Coard's research is particularly significant in examining disadvantage. Although dated, his work shows that Black pupils are made to feel 'educationally subnormal' for four main reasons: the idea that their language is second-rate and unacceptable in class; the association of 'white' with 'good' and 'black' with 'bad' in children's literature; poor and stereotypical representation of ethnic minorities in school textbooks; and racism from other students. Coard concludes that this inevitably leads to the self-fulfilling prophecy of underachievement.

Further evidence comes from the Jayleigh study which showed that within inner-city schools, ethnic minority pupils were at a disadvantage in terms of GSCE entries, being in lower sets and having to achieve higher grades in order to be perceived as successful. Wright's study found that some ethnic minority groups received poorer interaction from staff. Although Asian students were seen as 'good', Black students were seen as disruptive and disobedient.

This now takes up the alternative, critical positions, looking at factors pointing to institutional racism.

To return to the question, it must be made clear that not all students from ethnic minority groups underachieve. African and Afro-Caribbean girls achieve as many and often more qualifications than White students. Chinese students are also doing really well. It appears that factors such as class and gender are important here and, in terms of interactions between staff and students, some studies like Fuller's show that there is the possibility of resistance to labels and expectations.

The candidate makes a very important point at the start of this paragraph by arguing that not all ethnic minority students underachieve. This is an argument that many students fail to make and their responses assume that ethnicity means homogeneity.

This is an excellent response and worthy of 18 marks.

5

Meritocracy

Item A

Right-wing politicians often favour a return to the 1950s tripartite system, which they claim ensured genuine parental choice. However, many working-class pupils who 'failed' the 11-plus examination could only enter the secondary modern schools. From 1960 onwards the system was gradually replaced by the comprehensive system.

The Conservative governments of 1979 to 1997 were hostile to the comprehensive system, they wanted to offer choice and diversity without selection. They created new kinds of schools, such as grant-maintained and specialist schools with selection. Labour refuses to abolish grammar schools. It accepts selection by specialisation and parental choice. Tony Blair has attacked mixed-ability teaching, arguing that grouping children according to ability can be important in encouraging all pupils to progress as far as possible. In a class-divided society, however, such diversity and choice inevitably advantage the children of the powerful and articulate.

Source: adapted from Chitty, C. (1997) 'Choose...education?', *Sociology Review*, Vol. 6, No. 4.

Item B

The Marxist approach to education challenges the idea of a meritocracy. It assumes that in the 'race' for academic success, some students have more obstacles placed in front of them than do others. Some students barely start the race whereas others have so many advantages that they start much further down the track. These advantages are confirmed or reproduced by the education system.

(a) What is a 'meritocracy'? (Item **B**)   (2 marks)

(b) Identify and describe *two* advantages that some students may have over
   other students.   (4 marks)

(c) Suggest *three* reasons why some politicians may dislike the comprehensive
   education system.   (6 marks)

(d) Identify and briefly explain *two* reasons to show that the British education
   system is not meritocratic.   (8 marks)

(e) Examine the reasons why the school curriculum might advantage some
   students more than others.   (20 marks)

(f) Using material from Items **A** and **B** and elsewhere, assess the sociological
   arguments and evidence for the Marxist view that diversity and choice
   'inevitably advantage the children of the powerful and articulate'.   (20 marks)

Total: 60 marks

Answer to question 5: grade-C candidate

(a) A meritocracy is a system where you are rewarded for what you achieve and not for your family background.

> This is a good response and gains full marks.

(b) Some pupils' parents are teachers and therefore they know the school system well. They find it easy to talk to other teachers. Middle-class parents may pay for private tuition for their children so that they can get extra help with subjects that they find difficult. They will be more likely to get higher grades in these subjects as a result.

> The candidate has successfully identified and described two advantages and therefore gains full marks.

(c) Some politicians believe that standards have fallen in comprehensive schools. They prefer the grammar school system.

> The candidate has again identified one correct reason and therefore gains 2 marks.

(d) It is not a fair system because some children come from poor backgrounds.

> The candidate has identified but not explained one reason and therefore gains only 2 marks.

(e) Sociologists are critical of the National Curriculum because it is ethnocentric. This means that it treats White British culture as superior to other cultures. For example, English literature and history ignore the efforts and achievements of Black and Asian people. The 'great' authors we study in English are White men like Dickens, Wilkie Collins and Shakespeare. In history the only topic that pupils study in Black history is slavery in the Caribbean. This gives a very negative idea of Black people's history. Black pupils may feel very undervalued as a result of this and begin to resist and reject school.

> This is a sound beginning to the essay. The candidate has argued that the National Curriculum is ethnocentric and has provided some supporting evidence. However, it is important to note that the essay is on the wider curriculum as well as the National Curriculum.

In the past, girls were disadvantaged by the curriculum, especially in maths and science. There were hardly ever any maths examples with girls in them and in maths and science textbooks girls were hardly ever mentioned. This was one of the reasons why girls did not do as well as boys in these subjects and even dropped out of them before the exams. Spender said that girls received less attention from teachers than boys did. One sociologist said that some teachers even forgot the names of the girls in their classes because they were so quiet.

> Although this paragraph may sound commonsensical, the arguments are substantiated by sociological evidence and the candidate has made reference to Spender, even though this has not been developed.

Bernstein said that the language of middle-class students gives them an advantage in school because they use the elaborated code whereas working-class students use the restricted code. As schools use the elaborated code, middle-class students do better. Bourdieu also said that middle-class students have cultural capital.

> Some useful points, but the last sentence on Bourdieu needs development.

The curriculum can also refer to the hidden curriculum. This is everything you learn at school that is not on the timetable, e.g. obedience, punctuality and respect for teachers. Middle-class children tend to be seen as better students by teachers because of their manners and accents. Rist's study of the kindergarten showed how children were labelled by the head teacher on the basis of their dress and accents. This was seen as intelligence and is another way that the middle class children are advantaged.

> The reference to the hidden curriculum is relevant and a useful point is made — that it affects students in different ways. The example from Rist is rather simplistic.

In conclusion, having studied the evidence it is clear that the curriculum does not treat all groups the same. White middle-class children are much more at ease in school than Black boys.

> A fair conclusion, but the last sentence needs to be linked in.

> **Overall, a reasonable response which does focus on the question. It gains 13 marks.**

(f) According to the Marxist Clyde Chitty, in Item A, 'diversity and choice inevitably advantage the children of the powerful and articulate'. Marxists always argue that the education system benefits the children of the ruling class. Upper- and middle-class parents can afford to send their children to top public schools like Eton and Harrow. They are very likely to go on to Oxford or Cambridge University afterwards. Recently, a girl from a comprehensive school was refused a place at Oxbridge and the media blamed the universities for snobbism. Her school wasn't seen to be as good as a private school. Pupils from upper- and middle-class backgrounds are more likely to pass entrance exams for private schools because they have been better prepared for these tests.

> Although this paragraph could have been better structured, there is some useful material here. Again, the use of a relevant contemporary example is to be rewarded.

The Marxists Bowles and Gintis saw a correspondence between the needs of a capitalist society and the school. For them, schools were not organised to benefit all students but were meant to benefit the children of the middle and upper classes. The hidden curriculum taught most students to be obedient workers for capitalism. Another Marxist sociologist, Bourdieu, argued that middle-class pupils have cultural capital. This is a package of advantages which includes manners, respect

question

for teachers and accents that make teachers see middle-class pupils as more intelligent and more likely to succeed in school.

> Good use of Marxist references here, to show that the middle and upper classes benefit more from the education system.

In Item B it says that 'some students have more obstacles placed in front of them than do others. Some students barely start the race whereas others have so many advantages that they start further down the track'. Students who are articulate and from wealthy backgrounds are more likely to get into schools that do well in the league tables. Their parents can talk to the head teacher and they will do well in an interview for a school. In conclusion, it is clear from this discussion that the education system does benefit those pupils from upper-class and middle-class backgrounds.

> **The candidate makes use of Item B appropriately and has a reasonable understanding of the advantages that middle-class parents have in dealing with the education system. Overall, this is a good attempt, scoring 13 marks out of 20.**

■ ■ ■

Answer to question 5: grade-A candidate

(a) A meritocracy is a society where people's rewards and occupations result from their own merit — their efforts and abilities, not their social backgrounds.

> This is a well-expressed response and gains full marks. (What factors in a person's social background do you think might affect their success?)

(b) Two advantages that a student may have over others are attending the 'right' school and coming from a middle-class background. With league tables you can see that some schools get better results than others and attendance at these schools will be an advantage. Secondly, a middle-class background is more likely to advantage a student, as they are likely to have more cultural capital, which gives them a good start in education.

> Both of these are correct and gain full marks. Can you think of others?

(c) Three reasons why politicians dislike the comprehensive system are:
- they prefer selective education because they believe that the grammar schools offered a better education
- comprehensive schools are usually mixed-ability teaching and some people, like Blair, think this holds back the more able student
- the schools are often very big and they may become too impersonal for students

> These are three appropriate responses, for full marks.

(d) Firstly, it is not meritocratic because there is private as well as state education.

Therefore, some pupils gain a privileged route into the more prestigious universities and then into the professions.

Secondly, factors like class, ethnicity and gender all make a difference to achievement. If there was a meritocratic system, we would not see middle-class White girls doing better then working-class Afro-Caribbean boys.

e These are two clearly identified and well-explained responses, for full marks.

(e) However far the designers of a curriculum aim to make it a common cultural curriculum, it will always be more familiar to some social groups than to others. As we live in a multicultural, multiethnic and multifaith society, it seems unlikely that the curriculum could cater equally for this diversity.

e This is a very sophisticated introduction to the essay.

There are also factors of social class, language and gender which should be taken into account. Feminist sociologists like Spender have shown that in previous years, girls were given less attention in the classroom. Now we are looking for reasons why boys are not doing so well. The National Curriculum has included a coursework element in all subjects and some people argue that this gives girls an advantage because they have different study skills from boys.

e This paragraph sets out the structure for the rest of the essay. The candidate should now analyse and evaluate evidence and give explanations for such factors as social class, language and gender.

In terms of class, Nell Keddie showed that some knowledge is actually held back from some students, as teachers do not feel the students can cope with it. To belong to a lower working-class culture is also seen as an unlikely springboard for educational success. Bourdieu's work is relevant here as he says that the 'habitus' of the classroom eliminates the lower-class students. The curriculum from this viewpoint actually benefits the middle-class student.

e This is a very good paragraph on the problems facing working-class students in regard to the curriculum.

Ethnicity is another very important factor. Troyna and Cashmore pointed out that Christianity was emphasised in the National Curriculum at the expense of other faiths. Others like Wright have shown that teachers' expectations of some ethnic minority pupils lead to disaffection among pupils. Both Asian and Afro-Caribbean students were treated negatively. It is perhaps not surprising when very little of the curriculum relates to their life experiences. Asian languages do not get the status and respect of European languages like French and German. History is usually 'his-story' and about White superiority, therefore alienating girls and ethnic groups.

e This is a very good paragraph on ethnicity and the curriculum. The candidate has a sound grasp of relevant material and keeps the essay well-focused on the curriculum.

question

There seems to be little space within the curriculum to examine other cultures and beliefs in ways that give them equal credibility with White British culture and do not treat them as some exotic oddity. Troyna referred to the attempt at a multicultural curriculum as being little more than 'saris, steel drums and samosas'. So we can see that the school curriculum is not a neutral factor, but affects different students in different ways.

> This is an excellent essay, for 18 marks. The candidate has a sophisticated understanding of sociological explanations and a wealth of evidence to substantiate them. All the necessary skills are demonstrated.

(f) In Item A it says that as we are a class-divided society, the choice and diversity in education will inevitably benefit the children of the middle and upper classes. This is based on the Marxist view that the education system works in the best interests of the bourgeoisie.

> This is a good start. The candidate immediately uses material from Item A, as the question demands.

Since the 1980s, successive governments have claimed to increase both the choice and diversity in the education system. The Conservatives were responsible for diversity in secondary schooling because they introduced grant-maintained schools, city technology colleges and assisted places for state pupils to go to private schools. They claimed that this diversity would increase parental choice and it would also end the power of the LEAs.

> This paragraph sets the essay within a historical and political context, demonstrating good knowledge and understanding.

However, some Marxists argue that parental choice exists only for the middle classes who have a better knowledge of the schooling system as many of them have done well themselves. These parents are more likely to be able to afford to move to places where the catchment area is middle class and they can 'play the system' by getting their child into the school of their choice more easily than a working-class parent. This happened with the children of Prime Minister Tony Blair, because he was able to get his sons into the London Oratory even though it was a long way from their home.

> This is a good use of a contemporary example to make a point. It is always worthwhile using examples such as this because it shows examiners that you have an understanding of current affairs and that you can apply this sociologically.

Middle-class parents have what Bourdieu calls both economic and cultural capital. Economic capital has always allowed them to take advantage of diversity in education by buying places in private schools so that they get their children a more privileged education. Cultural capital means that within the state system, middle-class kids are more likely to pass entrance exams for selective schools and often use musical ability to get places in specialist schools. Once in the secondary school, the middle-class pupils are seen by teachers as more likely to succeed.

Marxists would claim that diversity and choice for the more powerful and articulate has resulted in 'sink schools' where there are very few middle-class pupils. Open enrolment has also meant that there is less diversity of ability within schools as the more able students are 'creamed off' into those schools high up the league tables.

The question uses 'inevitably', but we can see that not all working-class pupils fail. We can see that some succeed, although Marxists would say that this only justifies an unequal system.

The conclusion directly addresses the question and challenges the use of 'inevitably'. It is very important, as the candidate says, to show that not all working-class students fail in education but, as the Marxists argue, this may be a device to prove that the system is fair.

Overall, this is a very sound response, worth 18 marks.

Differential achievement

Item A

In *Racism, Gender and Young Children* (1998), Paul Connolly looked at social relations among very young children in a run-down, multicultural, inner-city neighbourhood. He used ethnographic research involving 5- to 6-year-olds. The stereotypes he found informed the ways in which teachers responded to children from different backgrounds — for example, older Black children were regarded as being disruptive and good at sport but not 'bright'. At the same time, while south Asian girls were categorised by teachers as the height of 'feminine' good behaviour, young White and Black children defined south Asian females as being 'alien' and unattractive.

Source: adapted from 'Education, inequality and identity', *Sociology Review*, Vol. 9, No. 1.

Item B

The role of the teacher as an agent of social control is extremely important in assessing the role of the hidden curriculum in maintaining gender inequality. Obviously, teachers' attitudes towards the role of education for women and men will influence their relationship with students. Spender found that in mixed classrooms, boys received two-thirds of teacher time, benefiting from the teacher's attention and detracting from the amount of time teachers spent with the girls.

Just as the attitudes of teachers can play a role in reinforcing gender inequalities through the hidden curriculum, so can the attitudes and behaviour of the students. A high level of sexual violence against females, both students and teachers, has been initiated by boys in mixed schools. Schools can be a system for legitimating male violence against women and for making this violence seem part of everyday life.

Source: adapted from Reynolds, K. (1991) 'Feminist thinking on education', *Social Studies Review*, Vol. 6, No. 4.

(a) Explain what is meant by the 'hidden curriculum' (Item B). (2 marks)

(b) Identify and describe *two* reasons why teachers may treat pupils from ethnic backgrounds differently from White pupils. (4 marks)

(c) Suggest *three* ways in which some ethnic minority students may respond to the negative labelling of them by teachers. (6 marks)

(d) Identify and briefly explain *two* ways in which a school may be seen as institutionally racist. (8 marks)

(e) Examine the similarities and differences between the functionalist and New Right approaches to education. (20 marks)

(f) **Using material from Items A and B and elsewhere, assess the extent to which school factors are responsible for the differential progress of boys and girls.** (20 marks)

Total: 60 marks

Task This question is for you to try yourself. You should spend some time researching suitable material and making notes, and then try to write the answer in 75 minutes — the time you will be allowed in the examination. Below are a few pointers to try to make sure that you are on the right track.

(a) Make sure that you have good knowledge and understanding of concepts related to education, in order to be able to answer this type of question.

(b) This question asks for reasons *why* teachers may treat pupils differently; it does not ask you to identify *how* they are treated. A possible reason may be that the teacher is expressing racism towards ethnic minority students.

(c) This question asks you to assume that there is negative labelling by teachers, so you need to think of some possible students' reactions. These might include forms of resistance as well as acceptance.

(d) For this question you must know the meaning of the concept. A useful way of learning concepts is to make a glossary for each of the sections in the topic. Lists of key concepts have been provided for you — you could revise these by providing the definitions.

(e) This is the first of the essay questions and it is important to note that the weighting here is 14 marks for knowledge and understanding with the remaining 6 marks for the other four skills. You *must*, therefore, make sure that you are demonstrating how much *knowledge and understanding* you have of these theories. Check back to the Content Guidance section (page 11 and pages 13–14).

(f) This essay reverses the weighting of assessment skills. You *must* use Items A and B and *clearly reference* them, for example 'as it says in Item B'. The question asks you to 'assess the extent' and therefore you must demonstrate *evaluation and analysis* here. You will find appropriate material on both in-school and out-of-school factors in the Content Guidance section (pages 16–17). It is important to write a conclusion for this type of essay as you will gain additional marks for evaluation.